Hilltop Elem. Library
West Unity, OH

My First REFERENCE LIBRARY

How WEATHER *Works*

Adapted from Theodore Rowland-Entwistle's *Weather and Climate*

ROBERT BROWN
JULIE BROWN

Gareth Stevens Children's Books
MILWAUKEE

For a free color catalog describing Gareth Stevens' list of high-quality children's books, call 1-800-341-3569 (USA) or 1-800-461-9120 (Canada).

Library of Congress Cataloging-in-Publication Data

Brown, Robert, 1961-
    How weather works / Robert and Julie Brown. — North American ed.
      p.   cm. — (My first reference library)
    Includes index.
    Summary: Introduces the elements that make up weather and climate, discusses methods of gathering data and forecasting the weather, and examines the climate's effects on animals and vegetation, and the effect of human activities on climate.
    ISBN 0-8368-0087-7
    1. Weather—Juvenile literature. 2. Climatology—Juvenile literature. [1. Weather. 2. Climatology.] I. Brown, Julie, 1962- . II. Title. III. Series.
QC981.3.B76   1991
551.5—dc20   91-2021

North American edition first published in 1992 by
Gareth Stevens Children's Books
1555 North RiverCenter Drive, Suite 201
Milwaukee, Wisconsin 53212, USA

Text and format copyright © 1992 by Belitha Press Ltd. and Gareth Stevens, Inc. Illustrations/photographs copyright © 1992 in this format by Belitha Press Limited and Gareth Stevens, Inc. US edition copyright © 1992. Conceived, designed, and produced by Belitha Press Limited and Gareth Stevens, Inc. First published in the United States and Canada in 1992 by Gareth Stevens, Inc. All rights reserved. No part of this book may be reproduced or used in any form or by any means without permission in writing from Gareth Stevens, Inc.

Photographic credits: Heather Angel, 38 (right); Aquila, 41 (right); Biofoto, 4; British Antarctic Survey, 57 (right); Canadian National, 15; John Cleare/Mountain Camera, 29 (left), 32 (left and right); Crown copyright, 17; Department of Electrical Engineering, University of Dundee, 12; Patrick Eagar, 8; ET Archive, 37; Sally and Richard Greenhill, 5 (bottom left); Susan Griggs/Comstock, 30, 31; Eric and David Hosking, 41 (bottom left); Hutchinson Library, 25, 39 (left), 51 (top) 53; G. V. Mackie, 16; Magnum, 39 (right), 42-43, 51 (bottom), 54, 58-59; S. & O. Mathews, 5 (top and center right); NASA, 57 (left); Oxford Scientific Films, 17, 43 (right); Panos Pictures, 59 (right); Photo Library of Australia, 36; Robert Harding Picture Library, 38 (left), 41 (top), 42 (left), 45 (top and bottom), 47 (bottom right), 52; Science Photo Library, 21, 28, 29 (right), 33, 34, 35; Charles Tait, 47 (top); ZEFA, 23

Illustrated by Oxford Illustrators Ltd. (Jonathan Soffe, Simon Lindo, and Ray Webb) and Eugene Fleury

Cover illustration by Howard Linton/Third Coast © 1990

Series editors: Neil Champion and Rita Reitci
Research editor: Scott Enk
Educational consultant: Dr. Alistair Ross
Design: Groom and Pickerill
Cover design: Beth Karpfinger
Picture research: Ann Usborne
Specialist consultant: Dick File

Printed in the United States of America

1 2 3 4 5 6 7 8 9 97 96 95 94 93 92

Contents

1: Weather or Climate?
What's the Difference? 4

2: The Weather Machine
What Makes the Weather? 6
Clouds 8
Rain, Hail, and Snow 10
Wind, Highs, and Lows 12
Storms 14

3: Weather Forecasting
Reporting on the Weather 16
Radar, Balloons,
     and Satellites 18
Putting It All Together 20
Reading a Weather Map 22

4: Climate
The World's Climates 24
Sea and Land............................26
The World's Winds 28
What Brings the Seasons? 30

What Makes a Climate?...........32
The Unquiet Sun 34
Volcanoes and Meteorites 36
Climate and Plants 38
Climate and Animals 40

5: Changes in Climate
Studying Climate Changes......42
Ice Ages 44
Climate in Early Times............46
Climate from the
     Middle Ages 48
The Moving Deserts 50

6: People and Climate
How People Change Climate ...52
The Greenhouse Effect 54
The Ozone Layer 56
Climate in the Future 58

Glossary............................60
Index..62

1: WEATHER OR CLIMATE?

What's the Difference?

Weather and climate are two ways of looking at changes in temperature, wind, rain, and sunshine. When we talk about weather, we mean the day-to-day changes in a certain place. Scientists who study weather are called meteorologists. When we talk about climate, we mean the usual weather of a certain place. Scientists who study climate are called climatologists. They believe it takes between 30 and 100 years to understand the climate of a place. Climate is

Those Circles

The lines on the map above are imaginary. Along the equator, day and night are always the same length. The Tropic of Cancer marks the point farthest north where the Sun appears directly overhead on June 21. The Tropic of Capricorn marks the southernmost place the Sun appears overhead on December 21. Inside the Arctic and Antarctic circles, there are days when the Sun never sets and other days when the Sun never rises.

different from place to place. For example, summers in southern California are always hot and dry, but in western Oregon, summers are often wet and cold. This difference is caused by the different climates.

Changes in Climate

Climates all over the world change with time. Only 20,000 years ago, ice covered large areas of Europe, Asia, and North America. In North America, the ice sheet reached as far south as the Great Lakes. Our climate is still changing today. Experts think that human actions, such as burning fossil fuels, may be causing some of the changes.

▲ Weather can change a lot in one day. Top: Oak trees photographed one April afternoon. Above: The next morning, there was snow on the ground.

◀ These two beach scenes were photographed at the same time of year but in places with different climates. One beach lies near the Arctic Circle, and the other lies in the tropics.

5

2: THE WEATHER MACHINE

What Makes the Weather?

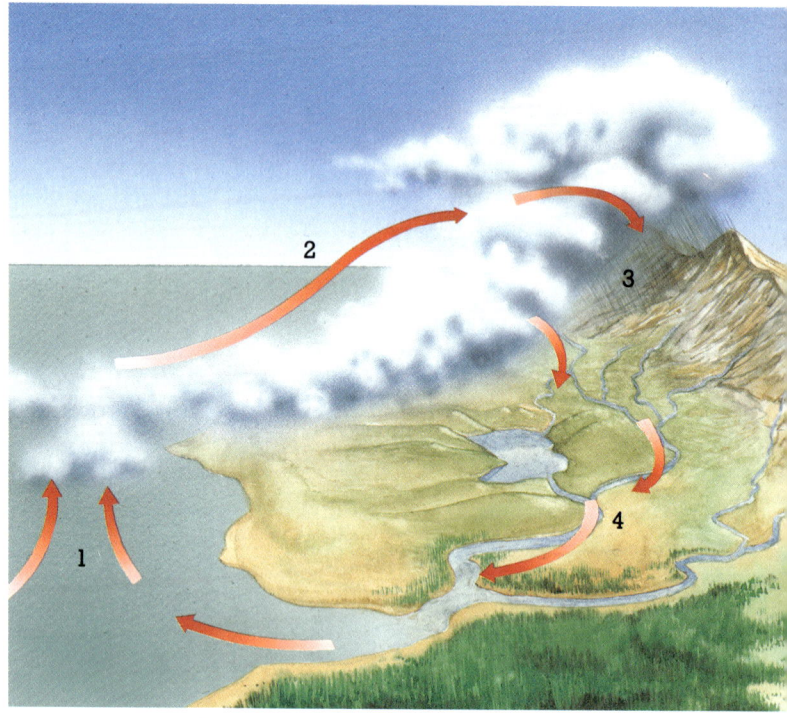

Water moves around the world in what we call the water cycle. Seawater evaporates (1) and forms clouds (2). Some of these clouds produce rain (3). If the rain falls on land, in time the water returns to the sea, for example, in rivers (4). ▶

Air Pressure

When air gets warm, it has less pressure. This means that changes in air temperature cause changes in air pressure. We use a barometer to measure air pressure. But changes in air pressure are not linked directly to rising and falling temperatures because the atmosphere is so complicated.

The weather is like something made by a machine. The Earth's air, or atmosphere, acts like the machinery, using sunshine as fuel. Because the Earth is round, the Sun's heat is hottest at the equator — it goes through the least amount of air. At the poles, sunshine goes through more air and spreads over more land, so there is much less heat.

Land and Sea

Land heats up and cools off more quickly than the sea does. In the tropics, land and sea are always very warm. Closer to the poles, the sea is cooler than the land in the summer but warmer than the land in winter. When the Sun heats the air, it also heats the sea. Some of the seawater evaporates — it rises into the air as moisture. When this moist air rises higher, it cools off. Then the moisture condenses, or turns into drops, forming clouds. If the clouds cool, the water in them makes larger drops or crystals that fall as rain, snow, or hail.

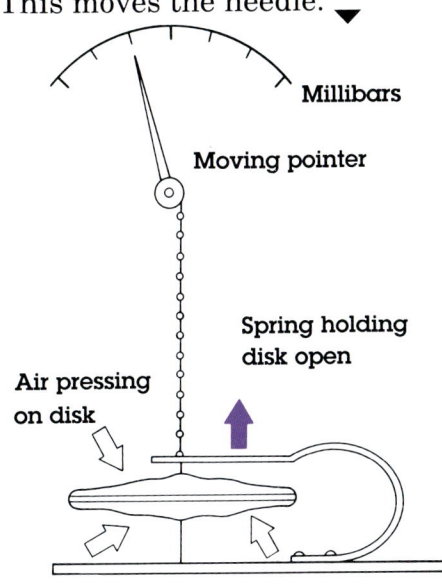

An aneroid barometer's disk shrinks or swells as air pressure changes. This moves the needle.

Did You Know?

Barometers are used to measure changes in air pressure. In a mercury barometer, a column of mercury in a glass tube rises and falls with air-pressure changes. Pressure is measured either in millimeters (of mercury in a barometer) or in bars. One bar equals 750.1 mm (29.53 inches) of mercury.

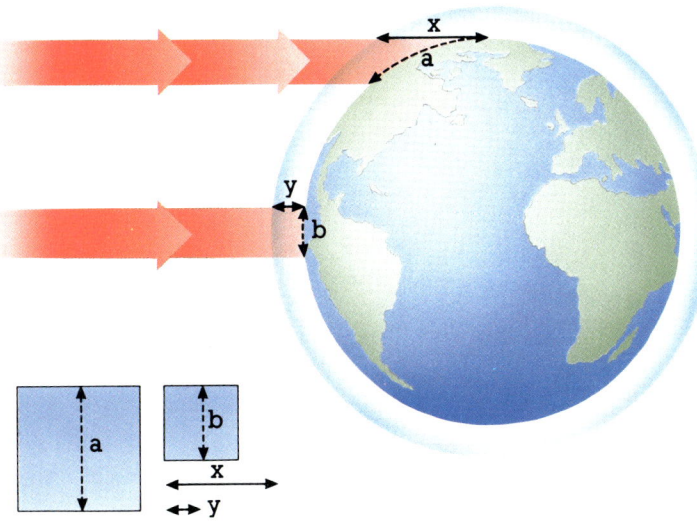

◀ The Sun's heat falls over more land at the poles (a) than at the equator (b). It also has to travel through more air at the poles (x) than at the equator (y).

THE WEATHER MACHINE

Clouds

Fog and Mist
Fog forms when water vapor condenses near the ground. Fog is made of millions of tiny water droplets, much the same as in a cloud. Mist forms in the same way as fog, but it is much less thick. Smog is fog mixed with particles of dirt, smoke, or chemicals.

During clear, calm nights, mist often forms in valleys. It often lasts even after the Sun rises.

When you boil water, it turns rapidly into vapor, an invisible gas. But under ordinary temperatures, water becomes vapor slowly. This is called evaporation. When heated air rises, it takes water vapor, or moisture, with it. As it rises, it grows cooler, and the vapor turns into water droplets. This is called condensation. In time, these droplets form into clouds.

Kinds of Clouds
The three basic cloud types are cirrus, cumulus, and stratus. *Cirrus* means "curl." Cirrus clouds look like wispy threads in the sky. They float as high as over 30,000 feet (9,100 m) above

◀ The five most common types of clouds. From top to bottom: high, streaky cirrus; patchy gray-white altocumulus; heavy cumulonimbus (thundercloud); cotton-ball-like cumulus; and gray, low-lying stratus, shown here veiling the Eiffel Tower.

Ten Cloud Types

Cirrus: high, white, wispy, feathery cloud.
Cirrocumulus: thin sheets of cloud forming ripples or patches.
Cirrostratus: thin, white, misty cloud.
Altocumulus: gray-white cloud in sheets or patches.
Altostratus: gray, streaky cloud that may cover the sky entirely.
Nimbostratus: thick rain or snow cloud, often dark; blots out the Sun.
Stratocumulus: rolling masses of gray or white cloud with dark parts.
Stratus: gray, low-lying clouds, usually producing drizzle; hides hilltops.
Cumulus: separate heaps of cloud rising high; often look like tufts of cotton.
Cumulonimbus: heavy, towering thundercloud.

ground. *Cumulus* means "heap." Cumulus clouds appear as great banks towering into the sky. *Stratus* means "layer," and stratus clouds form low gray layers. *Alto* means "high," and *nimbus* means "rain-bearing." These five words are combined to name ten types of clouds.

9

THE WEATHER MACHINE

A rainbow forms when the Sun shines on raindrops in the sky. Each raindrop acts as a tiny prism, breaking the sunlight into the colors of the spectrum.

Rain, Hail, and Snow

Coming Down

The biggest raindrops fall during summer thunderstorms. They can be a third of an inch (8 mm) across. The smallest drops are found in drizzle. The biggest snowflakes are up to two inches (50 mm) across. The heaviest hailstones ever reported fell in Ohio in 1981. Some weighed up to 30 pounds (13.6 kg).

Precipitation includes all forms of water that fall to the ground from the clouds. Meteorologists list eleven types of precipitation. But for most people, there are just three — rain, hail, and snow. All precipitation starts the same way — by ice particles or tiny water droplets joining together. It can take a million droplets to form one raindrop.

How Moisture Falls

As droplets grow larger, they become heavy enough to fall to the ground. Ice particles may melt and fall as rain, but if the air is cold they usually fall as snow or hail. Snow is more common in cold winter weather. Hailstones are heavy and fall rapidly, so they sometimes reach the ground still frozen, even in the summertime.

▲ Snowflakes always have six sides or six points, or sometimes both.

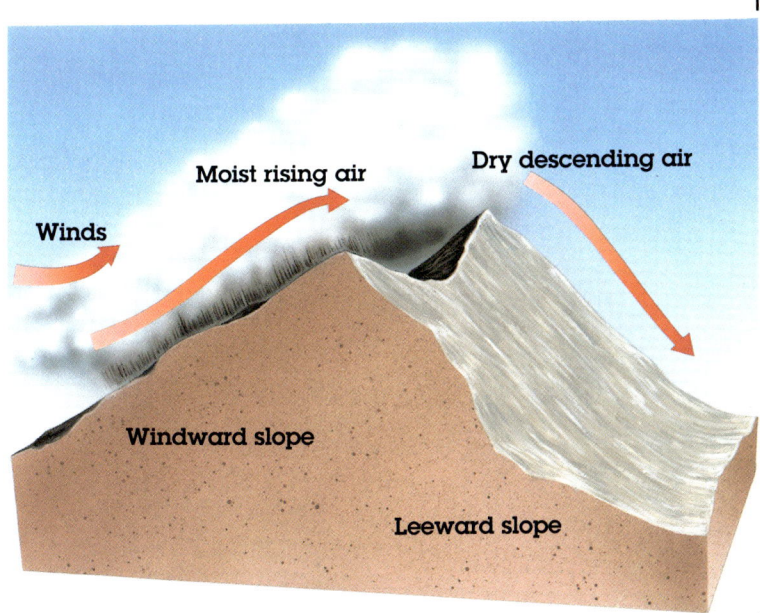

Rain Shadow

In western North America, most of the rain comes from the Pacific Ocean. West of the mountains along the coast, it is wet, but east of the mountains it is dry. This dry area is called a rain shadow.

Dew and Frost

At night, the Sun no longer warms the ground. Then, plants and other things on the ground may become cool enough for water vapor in the air to condense on them as drops of water. We call these drops dew. If it is cold enough to freeze, the water vapor will form a film of frost.

◀ The rain shadow. Rain falls on the nearest side of a mountain. The far side gets little rain and is much drier. This far side is said to be in a rain shadow.

Did You Know?

If rain seems to fall from a clear sky, the cloud has dissolved before the rain reaches the ground.

THE WEATHER MACHINE

Wind, Highs, and Lows

This picture from the US weather satellite *NOAA-9* shows two depressions, or lows, over western Europe. Depressions look like swirls of cloud. The cloud spirals are made by the way winds blow around the low. ▶

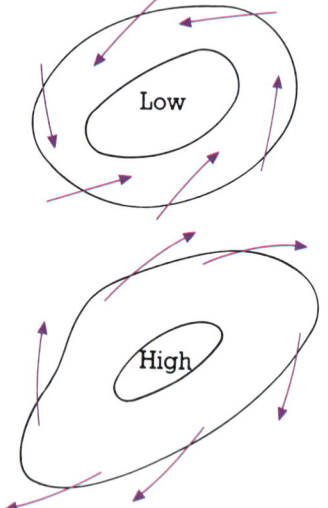

▲ Arrows show how the winds spiral clockwise around a high, and counter-clockwise around a low in the Northern Hemisphere.

Highs and lows bring different weather. Low-pressure centers are called depressions, cyclones, or just lows. Centers of high pressure are called anticyclones or highs. Lows usually have heavy clouds and strong winds.

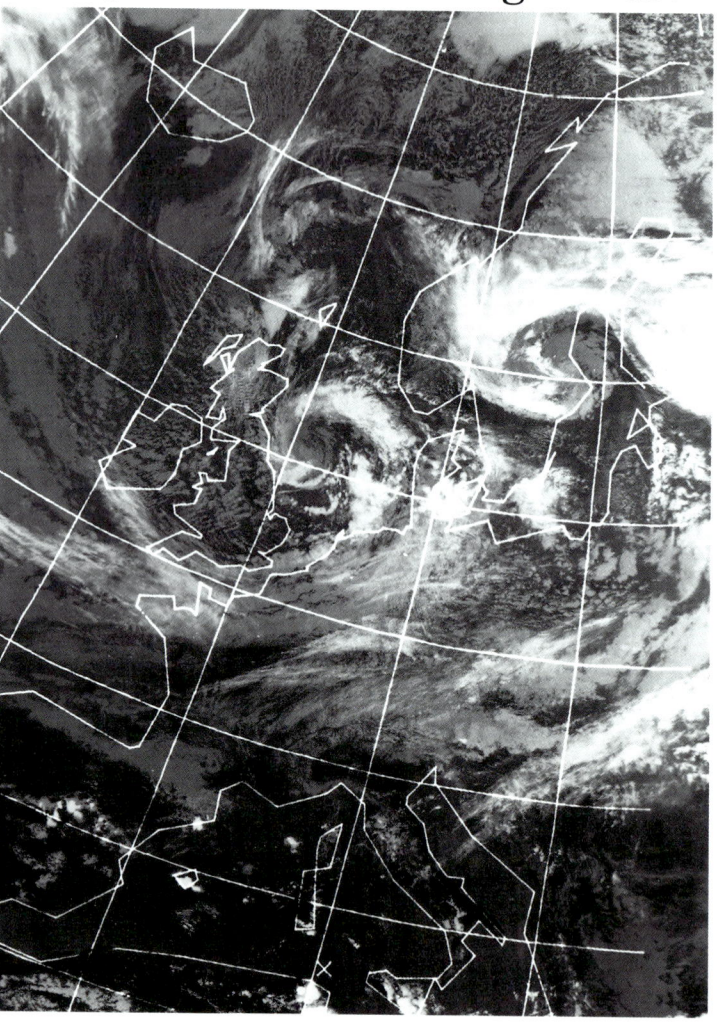

Lows bring rain or even storms. Highs have few clouds and light winds. In highs, you can usually expect good weather.

Veering and Backing

The wind does not blow evenly. Friction with the Earth's surface makes the wind gusty. Gusts are very uneven. Places over 300 feet (90 m) apart may have very different winds at the same time. When the wind is gusty, it usually changes direction. It can veer — change its direction clockwise — or back — change direction counterclockwise. In the Northern Hemisphere, winds over land tend to speed up and veer during the day and slow down and back at night. Over the open sea, winds do not change as much.

Coastal Breezes

In coastal areas, the wind usually changes direction between day and night. During the day, when the land is warm, cool air blows in from the sea. At night, when the land is cooler, the wind blows out to sea. It's easier for sailing ships to leave shore at night and return during the day. It's harder to leave shore when sailing against the wind.

During the day, warm air rises and moves out (dashed red line). Cool sea air moves onto land (yellow arrow). At night, the sea is warmer than the land, so the wind blows in the other direction. ▼

13

THE WEATHER MACHINE

Storms

A tornado can cause great damage by picking up and smashing cars, buildings, and people. ▶

Tropical storm diagram. Rising air (1) draws in air below (2) while the "eye" (3) stays calm. At the top, wind spirals out (4). ▼

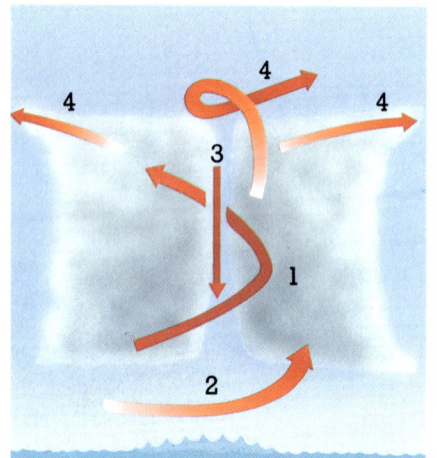

Did You Know?
The worst ever cyclone killed a million people in Bangladesh in 1970. The Tri-State Tornado, the US's worst, killed 689 people on March 18, 1925.

Winds grow strongest when a depression develops. Lows suck in air at the bottom, whirl it up and around, and hurl it out at the top. The steeper the low, the stronger the winds become.

Tropical Storms
Violent weather takes place in tropical storms. These develop over the sea, but they may move over land and do terrible damage. In the Caribbean Sea and the North Atlantic, these storms are called hurricanes.

14

They are called cyclones in the Indian Ocean, and willy-willies in Australia. In the northern Pacific Ocean, these storms are called typhoons. A tropical storm may be hundreds of miles wide, with winds blowing over 180 miles (290 km) per hour.

Tornadoes

A tornado is a funnel of wind that swirls around at up to 500 miles (800 km) per hour. It can suck up everything in its path, including buildings and cars.

Thunderstorms

Thunderstorms develop in dark, towering clouds. Violent currents of air rush up and down these clouds. Static electricity builds up in them. After a while, this static electricity produces a large spark, called lightning. Thunder is caused by the lightning heating the air suddenly. To find out how far away a lightning flash is, count the number of seconds between seeing the flash and hearing the thunder. Divide by five to get the distance in miles. To find the distance in kilometers, divide by three.

Lightning hits the CN Tower in Toronto.

3: WEATHER FORECASTING

Reporting on the Weather

If a weather forecaster wants to know what the weather will be tomorrow, he or she needs to know what the weather is like today over a wide area. If the forecaster wants to predict farther into the future, he or she will need weather information about a much larger area. A forecast for three or four days ahead needs information from the whole hemisphere!

Country Lore

Some sayings tell how to predict the weather, but like this rhyme, they are not always right:

*Red sky at night,
Sailor's delight;
Red sky in the morning,
Sailors take warning.*

A clear, red evening sky may mean good weather, and a cloudy, red morning sky may mean rain. But neither is always so.

An American groundhog, or woodchuck. Folklore in North America says that if the groundhog can see its shadow on February 2, then winter weather will last six more weeks. ▶

Getting Information

Wind, temperature, humidity, air pressure, cloud, rain, and snow information are needed to make a forecast. This information comes from ships, weather stations, weather balloons, and human watchers. Weather systems move all over the globe, often bumping together and overlapping. Predicting the weather farther than ten days ahead is nearly impossible. Wind and water often change direction suddenly in odd ways.

▲ A simple weather station recording temperature and humidity. The cover shades thermometers and lets air in.

This weather ship is recording changes in temperature, humidity, air pressure, and wind. ▼

17

WEATHER FORECASTING

Radar, Balloons, and Satellites

Meteorologists have many ways to collect weather information from up in the clouds and even far above them. Radar scanners constantly sweep the sky to find out about clouds and rain. Weather balloons filled with helium or hydrogen rise high into the sky, with instruments called sondes. These sondes sample the weather and then radio this information back to stations on the ground. Going up the highest of all are the

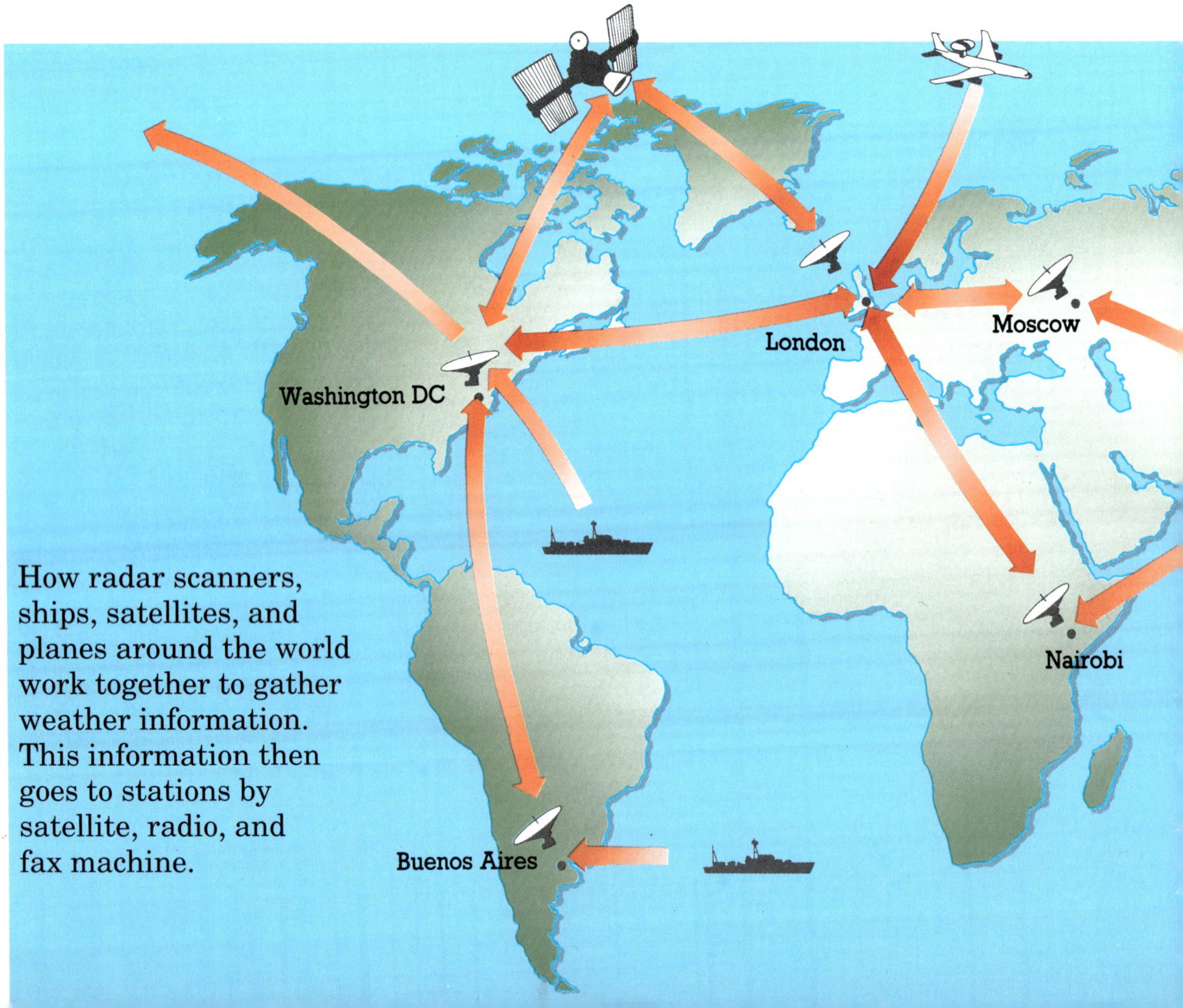

How radar scanners, ships, satellites, and planes around the world work together to gather weather information. This information then goes to stations by satellite, radio, and fax machine.

satellites. They orbit Earth and beam down pictures of weather systems. Pictures from these satellites can be seen on TV weather reports. Information about weather must be sent from one place to another very quickly, or it becomes useless. This is because weather changes so quickly. Meteorologists use communications satellites that are linked together so they can send information to and from distant places very fast.

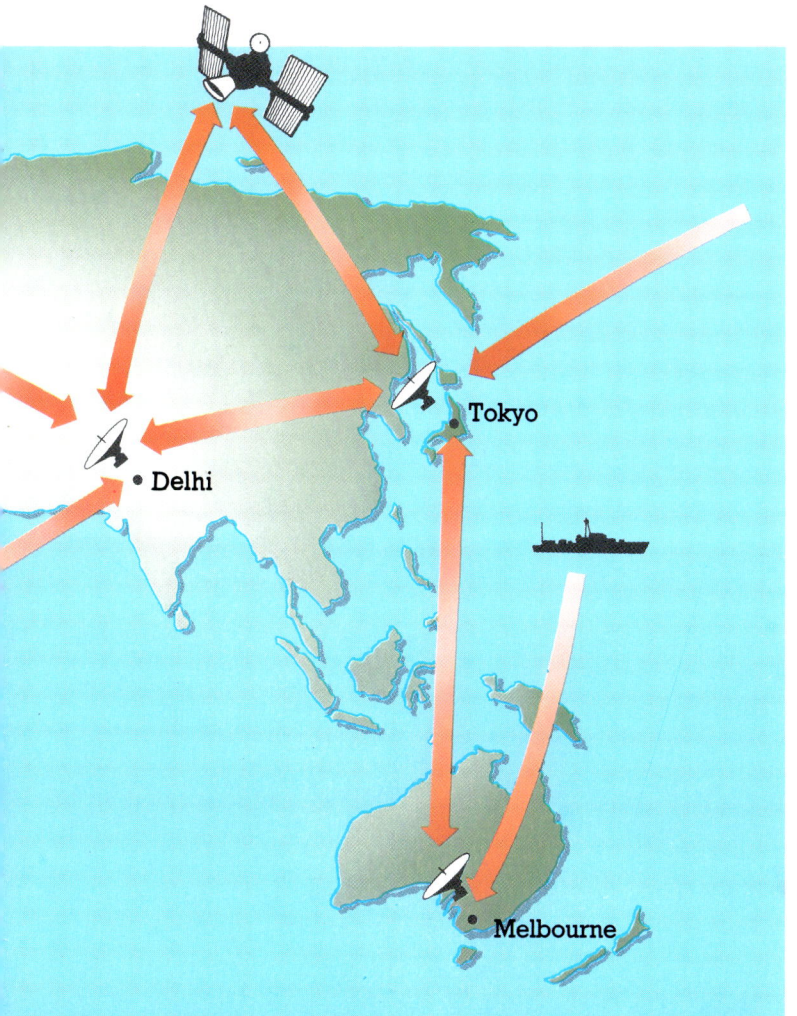

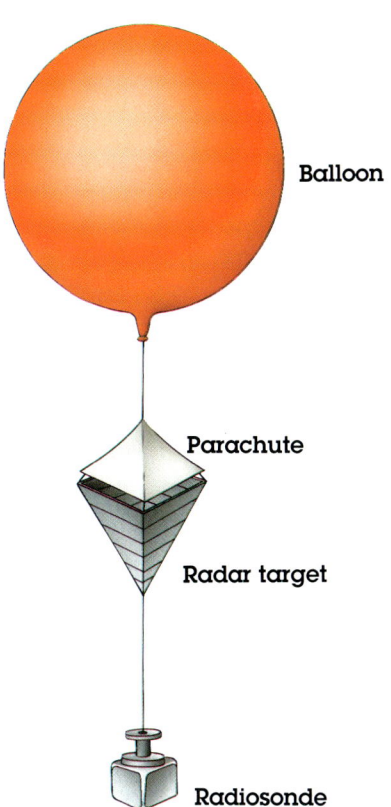

▲ A weather balloon carries a radiosonde that keeps track of the weather high above the ground. Its radar target helps radar follow the balloon. When it gets too high, the balloon bursts, and the sonde floats down on its parachute. The sonde can be recovered and used again.

Computer Link

All the major weather centers are linked into a large computer network. The network quickly sends information around the world.

19

WEATHER FORECASTING

Putting It All Together

This flow chart shows how all the information about the weather is gathered together to bring you the daily forecast. ▶

Points of equal pressure are plotted on a map. These points are then joined by lines called isobars. These numbers are in millibars. ▼

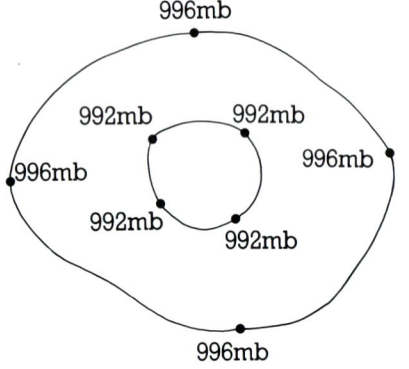

Human beings can work out a prediction for the weather in a small area for the next 18 hours. But for a larger area or a longer time, they must use computers.

Figuring It Out
The way highs and lows move show changes of wind direction, and these may show changes in temperature. The computer can figure where the changes will be and print them out on a chart.

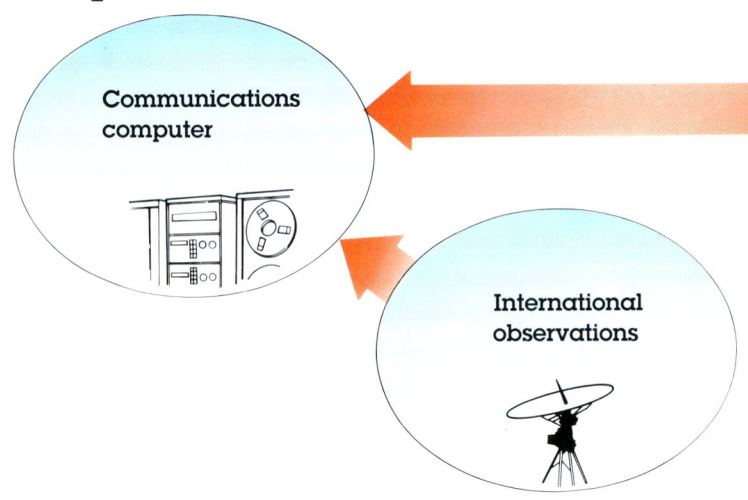

Then areas that have the same air pressure are joined with lines called isobars. The forecaster looks at the isobars and also at recent satellite photographs of clouds. Then the forecaster decides what may happen next.

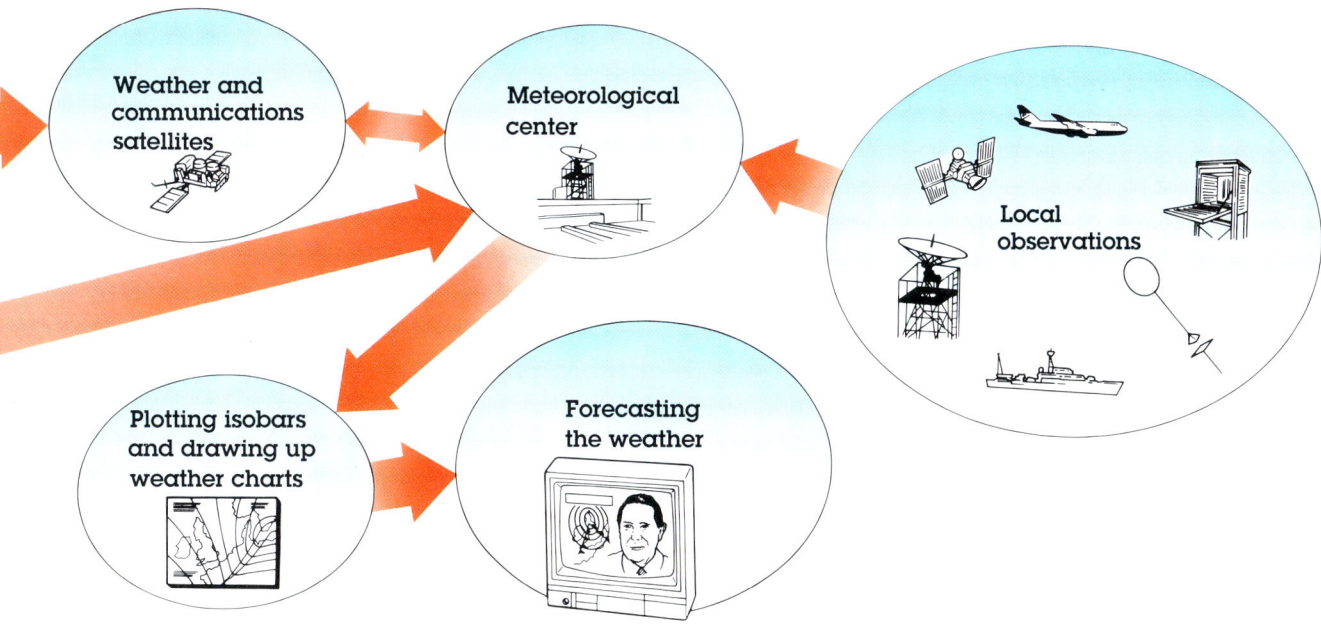

Weather forecasting is not easy. But predictions are right most of the time. When they are wrong, it's usually because the timing is wrong. Rain may come earlier or later than the forecast said.

▲ Top: A forecaster at work. The computers give him information from around the world.

WEATHER FORECASTING

Reading a Weather Map

A weather map of northwestern Europe. In the west, there are centers of low pressure, clouds, rain, and winds. In the east, high pressure leads to clear skies. The key below the chart helps us read the symbols. Wind speeds are given in knots, or nautical miles per hour. ▶

Special Forecasts

Some people need special weather information. Farmers need to know weather conditions that favor pests, or if a coming storm means getting their livestock to safety. Gas companies need to know when it will be cold so they can supply people with fuel. Ships and airplanes need to know how the weather will affect their journeys.

A weather map may look complicated, but anyone can learn to read one. To find the areas of high and low pressure, look for the isobars. Closely spaced isobars mean a low, usually with wind and rain. Widely spaced isobars mean a high, usually bringing clear weather. But in winter, a high may mean frost or fog.

Fronts	Cloud Amount	Weather
Warm front	Full cover (overcast)	Rain
Cold front	3/4 cover	Drizzle
Occluded front	1/4 cover	Showers
		Mist

Winds
5 knots
10 knots
15 knots
20 knots

Figures above the "cloud" symbols are temperatures in degrees Celsius

Isobars are labeled in millibars

22

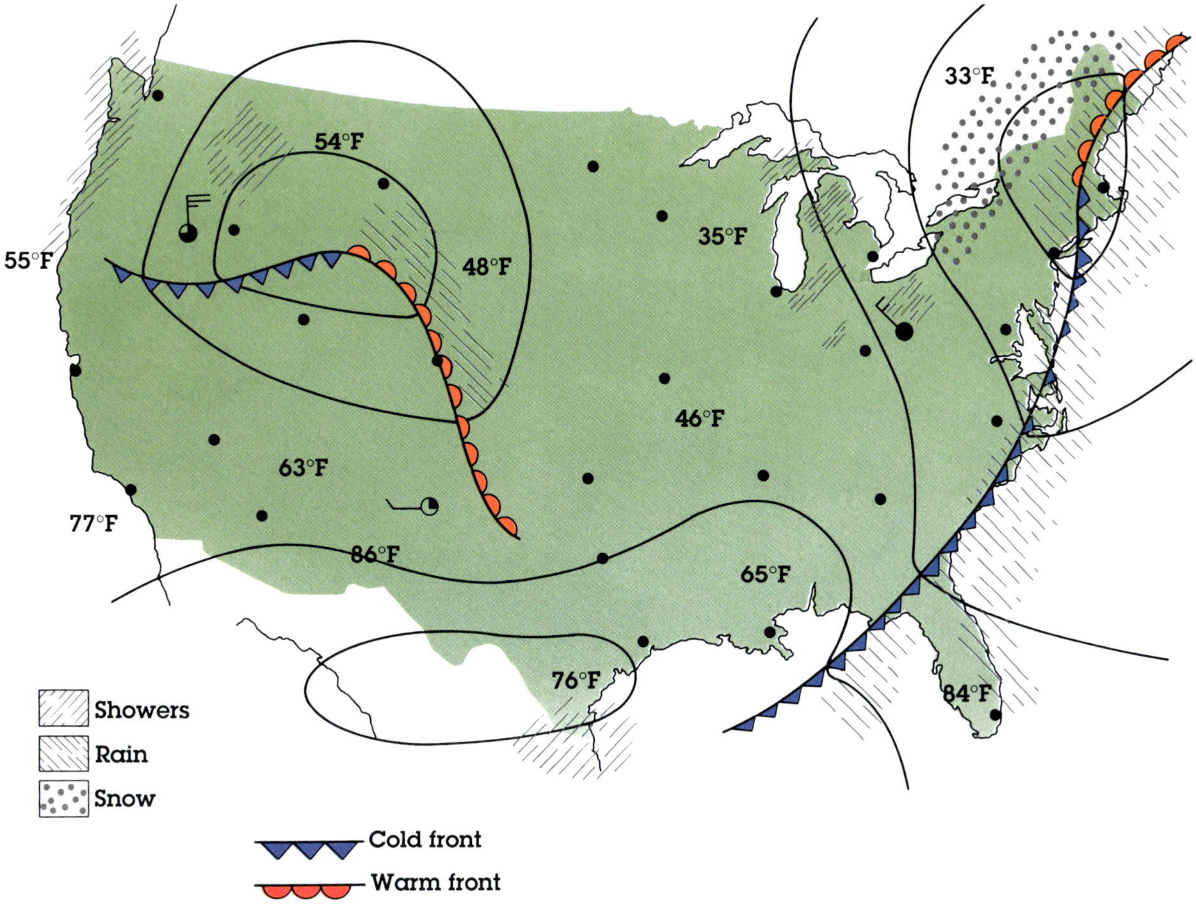

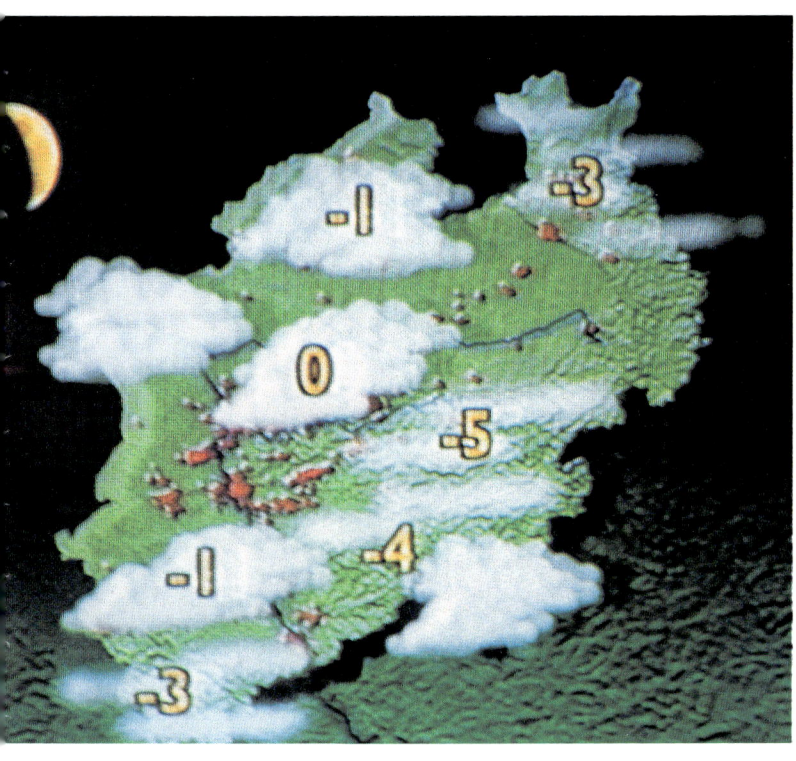

▲ A map showing weather in the United States for a day in April. The East Coast has rain in connection with a cold front. In the Northeast, we see snow as a result of low pressure and a warm front. In the Southwest, there is an area of high pressure, with high temperatures and clear skies. In the Northwest it is cooler, with rain.

◀ TV forecasters explain their predictions with simple weather maps like this one for an area in Germany.

23

4: CLIMATE

The World's Climates

Climate controls the kinds of plants and animals that live in a certain area. Climate affects the way people live, dress, and work. And over thousands of years, people's bodies have changed to suit their climate.

Climates can be classed into 12 basic types. They are listed in

Main Climate Types

Icecap: always freezing; sometimes it snows.

Polar: cold and dry; short, chilly summers.

Subarctic: long, cold winters, short, cool summers; some moisture.

Steppe: great changes from hot to cold; little precipitation.

Highlands: cooler than the surrounding areas.

Continental moist: cold winters; warm summers; moderate precipitation.

Oceanic moist: cool winters, warm summers; moderate precipitation.

Desert: great change from hot during day to cold at night; little rain.

Subtropical dry summer: mild, wet winters; hot, dry summers.

Subtropical moist: cool winters; warm to hot summers; moderate rain.

Tropical wet and dry: hot, with dry and very wet seasons.

Tropical wet: hot and wet all year round.

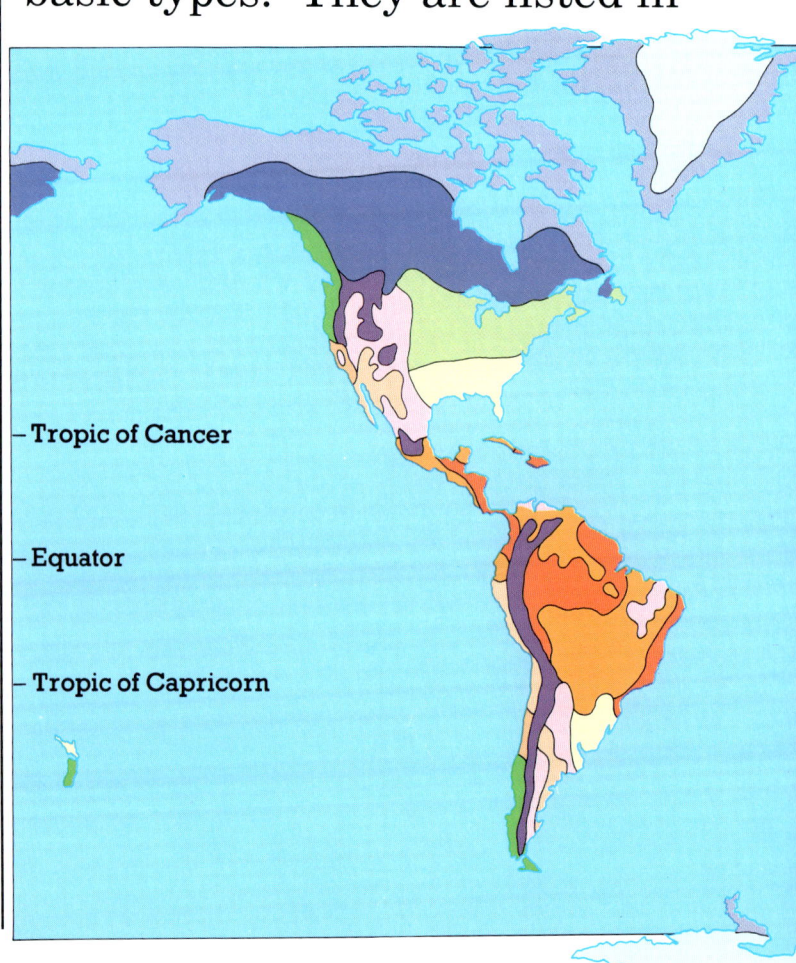

24

the panel on the left. Climates range from cold and dry at the polar ice caps to hot and wet near the equator. Each climate zone has differences within it. Minnesota has long, cold, snowy winters. But Maryland has shorter and milder winters, with little snow. Kenya is a country in Africa that lies across the equator. Its coast is hot and humid, its highlands are much cooler, and Mount Kenya, its highest mountain, has glaciers.

▲ Mount Kenya lies near the equator, but it is always capped with snow. This shows how a climate can have many differences within it.

Protective Coloring

People who live in hot climates, such as Africa, the Pacific islands, and the Mediterranean area, tend to have dark skin. Their dark skin protects them from the harmful rays of the Sun.

◀ The world's climatic regions. On the opposite page is a key to this map. Even though the equatorial region gets the most heat from the Sun, the main desert areas lie well north and south of the equator.

25

CLIMATE

Sea and Land

This map shows the world's main warm and cold ocean currents. These currents are caused by cold polar water moving toward the equator and warm tropical water moving away from the equator. ▼

Water heats up and cools off more slowly than land, so seacoast areas have smaller changes in temperature than inland areas. Ocean currents can affect coastal areas. Surface ocean currents come from the Earth's rotation, wind, and tides. Deep currents flow from cold polar areas toward the equator.

The Gulf Stream

The warm Gulf Stream flows from the Gulf of Mexico northeast to Europe. This current

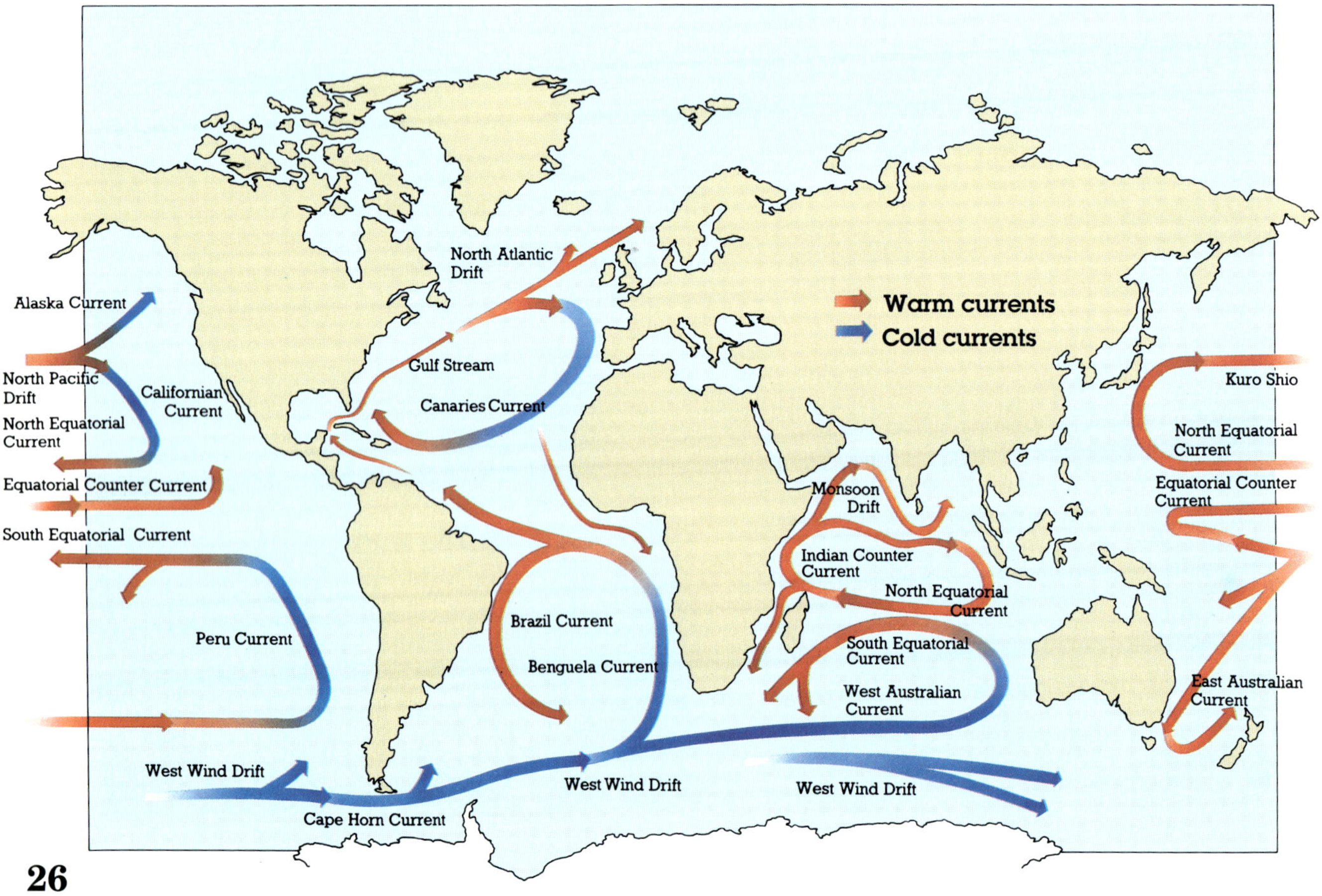

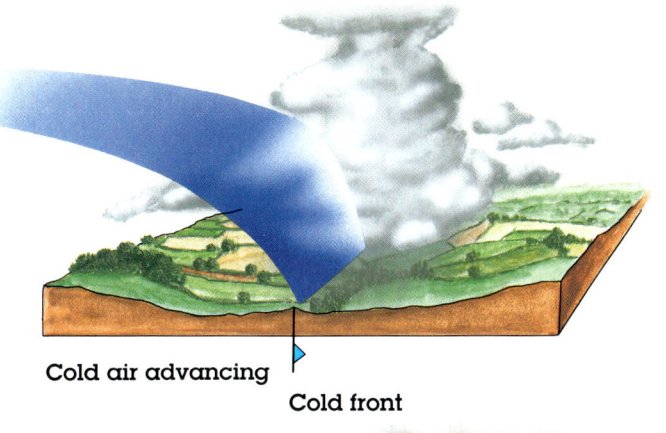

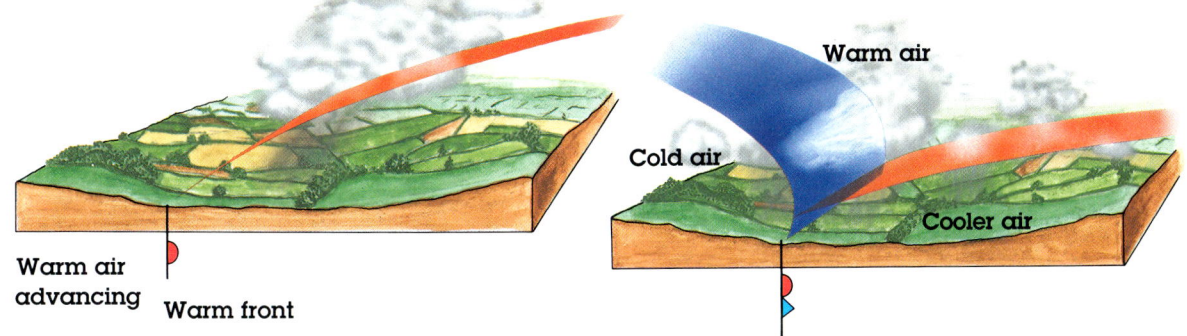

Occluded front

▲ Three types of fronts and their symbols. A front is a new air mass pushing out an older one. Cold fronts usually bring rain followed by clear skies. Warm fronts bring low clouds and maybe rain or snow. Occluded fronts may bring rain, but their outcome is very hard to predict.

Currents Flow

When people talk about the direction of an ocean current, they mean the direction toward which the current flows. So a southerly current flows from north to south.

warms the coasts of Iceland, the British Isles, France, and Norway.

Air Masses

Large amounts of air, known as air masses, can be warm or cold, depending on where they come from. In the United States, air masses from Canada tend to be cold, while air masses from Mexico tend to be warm. The boundary between two air masses is called a front. Warm air moving in is a warm front. If cold air enters, it is a cold front. A cold front pushing up warm air and facing cold air is called an occluded front.

El Niño

El Niño, a warm Pacific current, can change our weather. At times, it blocks the flow of cold water north from the Antarctic. This causes drought, storms, and floods in areas that usually don't have them.

27

CLIMATE

The World's Winds

The world's major wind zones. The doldrums and horse latitudes are regions of calms, but storms can still blow up. ▶

▲ An anemometer, like this one at an observatory in England, measures wind speed.

In some areas of the Earth, winds may blow continually. They are known as prevailing winds. Over about 500 miles (800 km) on each side of the equator lie the doldrums — calm areas without prevailing winds.

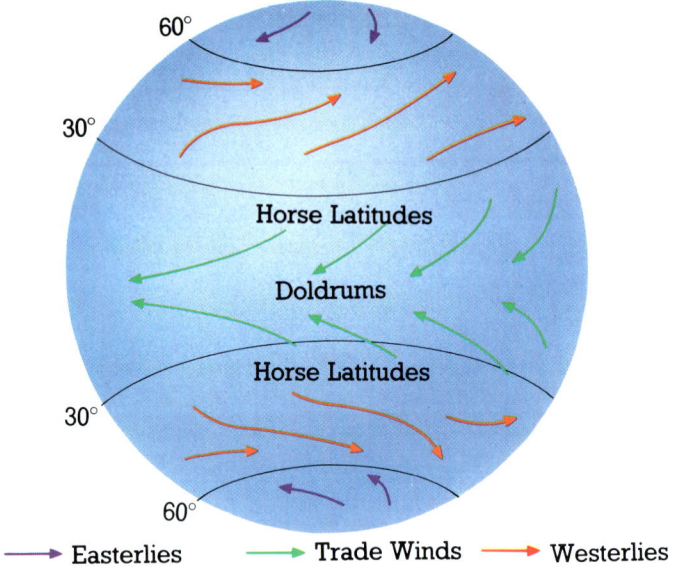

→ Easterlies → Trade Winds → Westerlies

On either side of the doldrums are two regions of trade winds. They blow toward the equator and slightly east. Sailing ships used to rely on the trade winds for power. At a distance of 30° latitude on both sides of the equator lies a belt of calms called the horse latitudes. North and south of the horse latitudes lie the prevailing westerlies. They usually blow west and toward the poles, but can change

◀ Strong prevailing winds blowing from the right made these trees grow into a bent shape.

Winds Blow

Wind directions are always given from where the wind is coming from. So westerlies blow from the west. Currents are named the other way.

from day to day. The prevailing easterlies around the poles blow east and outward from the poles. An anemometer measures wind speed. It has cups on spokes that spin in the wind. Gears link the cups to dials that tell how fast the wind makes the cups spin.

▲ These clouds in a jet stream over Egypt and the Red Sea were photographed from a US spacecraft.

The Beaufort Wind Force Scale

Wind speed is indicated by force numbers from 0 to 12. The scale given here is the one used on land. British admiral Sir Francis Beaufort invented the wind force scale in 1805.

No.	Name	Speed in mph (kph)	Effects of wind
0	Calm	Under 1 (<1)	Smoke rises straight
1	Light air	1-3 (1-5)	Smoke shows wind direction
2	Light breeze	4-7 (6-11)	Wind felt on face
3	Gentle breeze	8-12 (12-19)	Paper and dry leaves move; flags fly out
4	Moderate breeze	13-18 (20-28)	Dust and small branches move
5	Fresh breeze	19-24 (29-38)	Flags flap; small leafy trees sway
6	Strong breeze	25-31 (39-49)	Large branches sway
7	Moderate gale	32-38 (50-61)	Whole trees sway
8	Gale	39-46 (62-74)	Difficult walking into wind; twigs break
9	Strong gale	47-54 (75-88)	Branches on ground; shingles blow off
10	Storm	55-63 (89-102)	Trees fall; buildings heavily damaged
11	Violent storm	64-73 (103-117)	Widespread damage
12	Hurricane	Over 73 (>117)	Buildings destroyed

Jet Streams

Jet streams are fast air currents, usually between 27,000 and 45,000 feet (8,000-14,000 m) high. They can travel up to 300 miles (480 km) per hour. They can speed up or slow down a plane flying in or near them. Two major jet streams flow west to east in each hemisphere, and one near the equator flows east to west.

29

CLIMATE

What Brings the Seasons?

Below: A New England countryside in summer, when the tree leaves are green. Opposite: The same scene in the fall, after the leaves have changed color. ▼

Our planet's movements bring us the seasons. Earth circles the Sun once a year. At the same time, it spins on its own axis, like a top. Earth is always tilted at about 23.5°. This makes different parts of our planet get more sunlight than other parts at certain times of the year. When the North Pole is tilted toward the Sun, the Northern Hemisphere gets more sunshine and has summer — and the Southern Hemisphere has its winter. When the South Pole is tilted toward the Sun, the Northern Hemisphere gets less sunshine and has winter — and the Southern Hemisphere can then enjoy its summer.

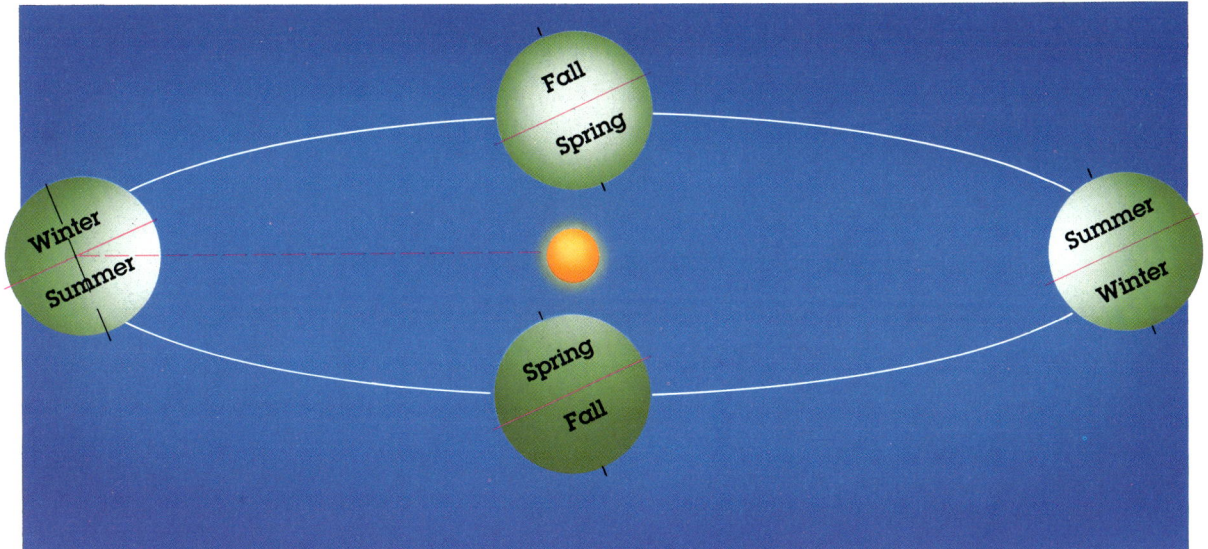

Day and Night

Every 24 hours, Earth makes one turn. When our half faces the Sun, we have day. When our half turns to face darkness, we have night. In most places, days are shorter in winter and longer in summer. Long nights help make the weather colder.

▲ The tilt of the Earth, showing how different places get more sunshine during the year while the planet is circling the Sun. This produces the changes in temperature that we call seasons. When the Northern Hemisphere has summer, the Southern Hemisphere has winter.

CLIMATE

What Makes a Climate?

There are many reasons why climates are different from place to place. Climates result from the Earth's surface being heated by the Sun and then cooling down at night. The Earth gives off some of the heat it got from the Sun. The amount of heat a place has kept or lost is called the radiation balance.

Gains and Losses of Heat

The Earth receives the most sunlight at the equator, and this amount gets less toward the poles. The atmosphere also affects incoming and outgoing

This mountain pass was photographed on the same day on both sides. Left: The slope facing north is snow-covered. Right: The slope facing south is warmer and does not have any snow. ▼

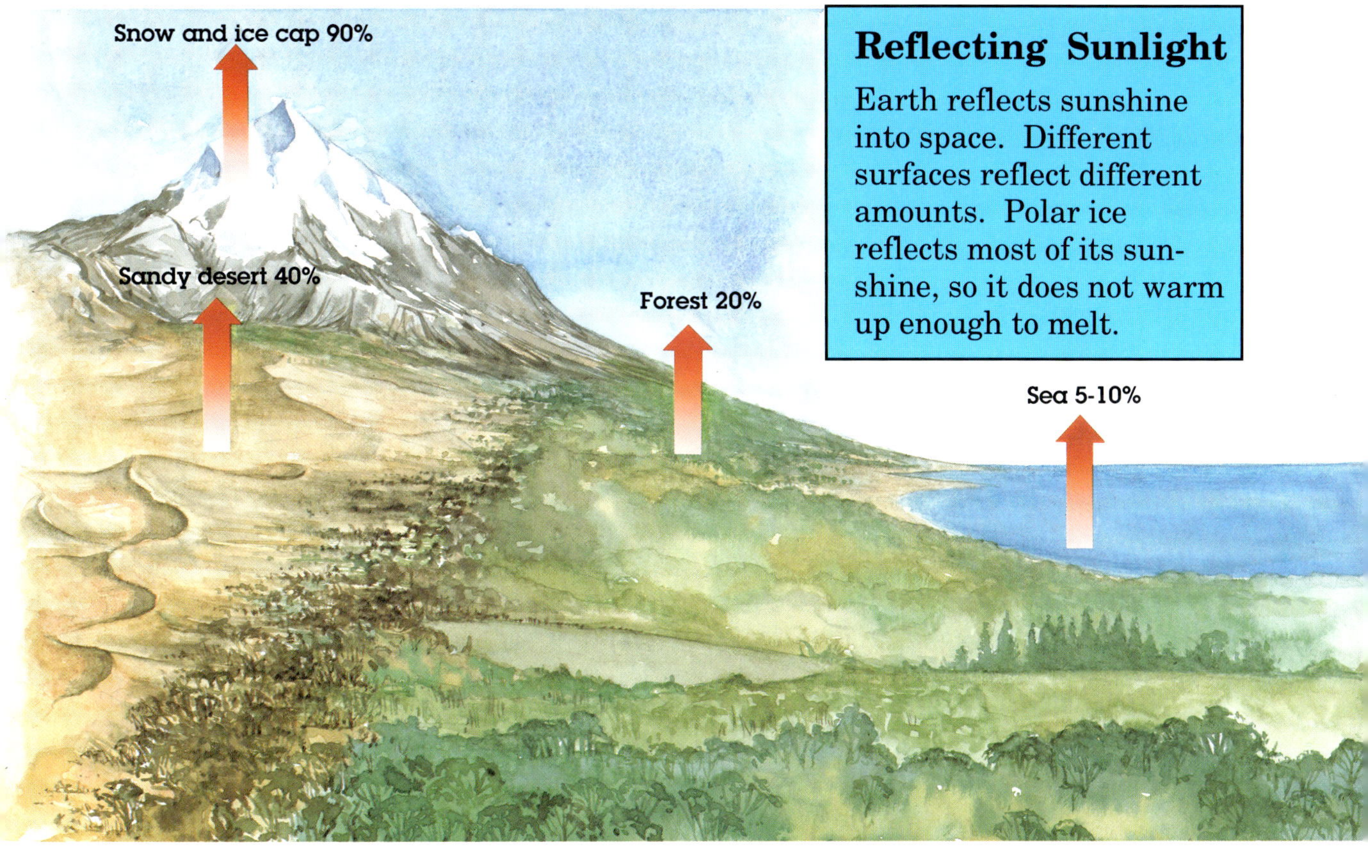

Snow and ice cap 90%

Sandy desert 40%

Forest 20%

Sea 5-10%

Reflecting Sunlight

Earth reflects sunshine into space. Different surfaces reflect different amounts. Polar ice reflects most of its sunshine, so it does not warm up enough to melt.

▲ The percentage of sunlight reflected by several different surfaces.

heat. The Sun shines more, and warmer, through clean air than it does through polluted or cloudy air. Oceans store heat, making coastal climates warmer than those inland. Sea currents warm or cool the air. The wind's direction affects both rainfall and temperature. Land that slopes southward in the Northern Hemisphere gets more of the Sun's heat. Plants will grow better there. In the Southern Hemisphere, land sloping northward is warmer.

A solar power station in Italy. Long sunny hours can generate plenty of electricity. ▼

CLIMATE

The Unquiet Sun

The Earth's elliptical orbit around the Sun. Its distance from the Sun changes with its place in the orbit. ▼

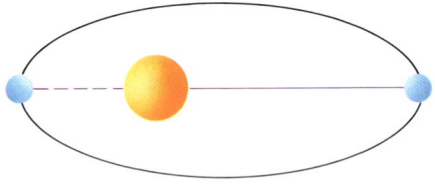

--- Distance at perihelion
— Distance at aphelion

Skylab photographed the Sun's ever-changing surface. The Sun is a ball of gases, and it produces energy from nuclear fusion reactions. The glowing red loop of gas you see reached a temperature of 36,000°F (20,000°C)! Water boils at only 212°F (100°C). ▶

The Sun does not give off a steady flow of heat. There are several reasons for this. The Earth's orbit around the Sun is a flattened circle called an ellipse, so sometimes the Earth comes closer to the Sun (perihelion) and sometimes it is farther away (aphelion). The tilt of the Earth can change over thousands of years, and this also can change our climates.

Sunspot Activity

The Sun sends out a stream of particles, called the solar wind. The solar wind's force changes. It is strongest during sunspot activity. Sunspots are dark patches that appear on the Sun's surface every few years. The

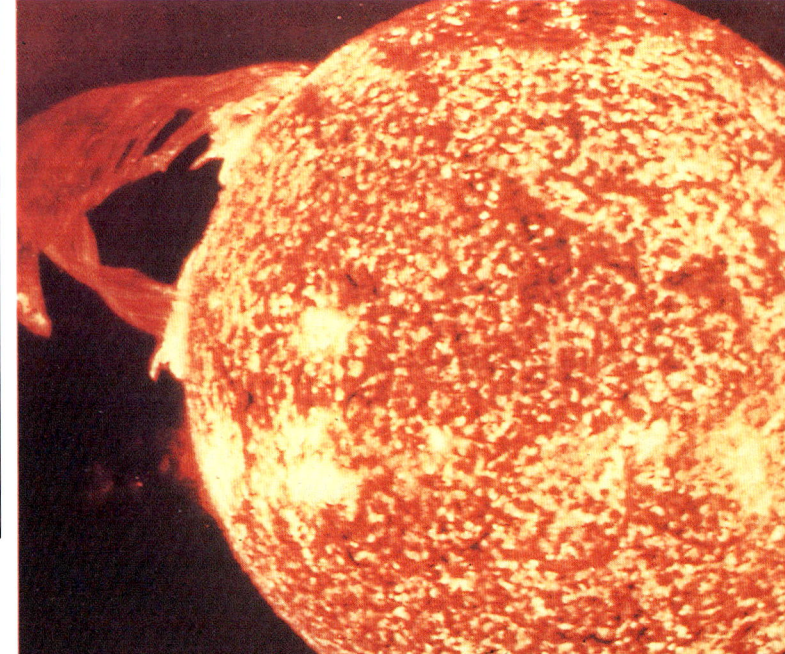

34

◀ The aurora borealis, or northern lights, seen in the Alaskan sky. These beautiful lights result from tiny particles with electrical charges that enter Earth's atmosphere. The North and South poles are magnetic, so they attract the most particles. People in the Southern Hemisphere can see the aurora australis, or southern lights.

Sunspot Facts

The Sun has a magnetic field, and changes in this field cause dark patches to form on its surface. These patches are known as sunspots. The number of sunspots rises to a peak every 11 years. They can cause trouble for radio and television broadcasts and for magnetic compasses.
Warning: Never look at the Sun without special equipment. You could go blind. Dark glasses and smoked glass will not protect your sight.

number changes regularly. Less rain usually follows a time of very many sunspots. Every one or two centuries, the number of sunspots suddenly gets much larger. This can result in a change of climate. Because the Sun affects our climate, we need to study it to learn what may happen to the weather on Earth.

CLIMATE

Volcanoes and Meteorites

This huge crater in Australia may have been made by a meteor striking the Earth millions of years ago.

Near Misses
Thousands of asteroids — rocky bodies — orbit the Sun. Recently, two of them nearly hit Earth. In 1937, Hermes, a mile (1.6 km) wide, came very close. In 1989, another asteroid swerved near us.

An erupting volcano sends red-hot lava streaming down its sides. Lava is the erupted form of magma, the molten rock that exists miles down inside the Earth. A volcano also hurls forth clouds of ash, gas, steam, and dust, and lumps of rock.

When a volcano erupts, it shoots out gases and ash that can make the sky hazy. Experts think that clouds of volcanic ash can block the Sun and cool the climate. In 1835, Cosigüina, in Nicaragua, erupted and threw out 4.8 cubic miles (20 cu km) of dust! Mount St. Helens, in the state of Washington, exploded in 1980. It took months for the local people to clean the ash from their houses and yards.

Missiles from Space
Meteorites — objects that come from space — can cause even bigger dust clouds. In northern Arizona, a prehistoric meteorite dug the Barringer Meteor Crater. Some scientists believe that dust clouds, created by a meteorite and blocking sunlight for years, may have killed off the dinosaurs.

◀ A picture by Joseph Turner (1775-1851), an English artist famous for his sunset paintings.

Turner Sunsets

Joseph Turner lived and painted sunset scenes in the 1800s, after Cosigüina erupted. Volcanic dust may have caused those beautiful sunsets that he depicted.

CLIMATE

Climate and Plants

- ■ Coniferous forest
- ■ Mediterranean scrub
- ■ Temperate broad-leaved forest
- ■ Equatorial and tropical rain forest
- ■ Grassland
- ■ Semidesert
- ■ Desert
- ■ Tundra and alpine
- ■ Ice desert

▲ Alaskan tundra, with mosses and sedges.

Coniferous evergreen forests in cooler areas. ▼

Tropical rain forests grow in hot, wet places. ▼

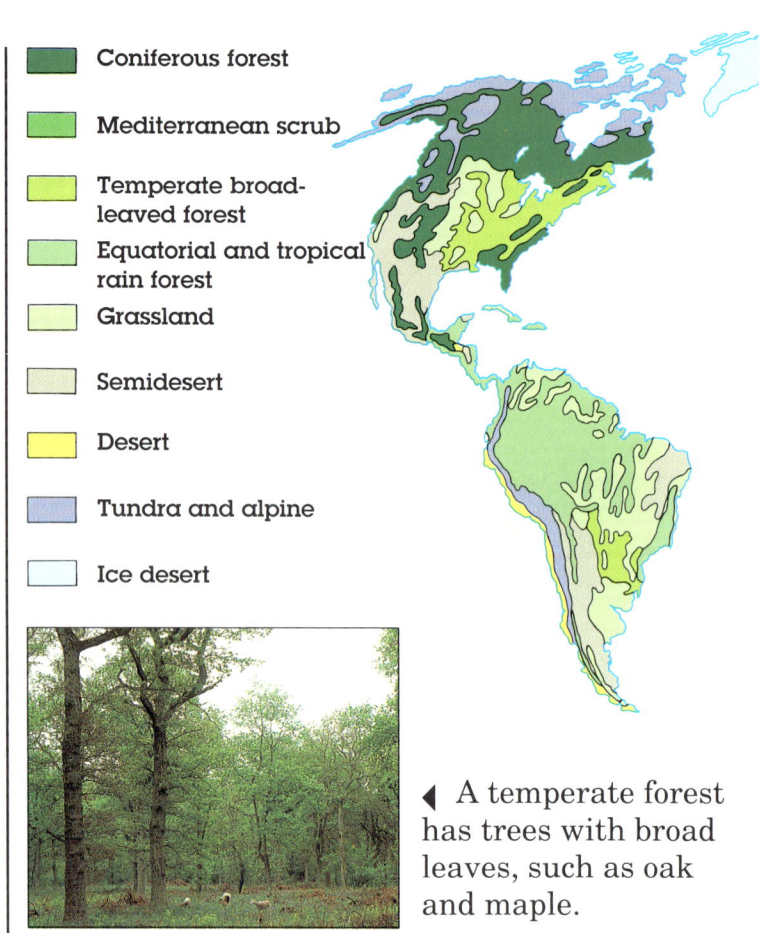

◀ A temperate forest has trees with broad leaves, such as oak and maple.

Climate controls which plants and animals can live in an area. Far north in the tundra, only moss and plants with short growing seasons can thrive. Animals travel there to eat in the short summer. Far south lies icy Antarctica, where few plants can grow — enough to feed the spiders and insects that live there. Between the polar circles and the tropics, the climate is warmer. Forests and prairies grow well there. In the

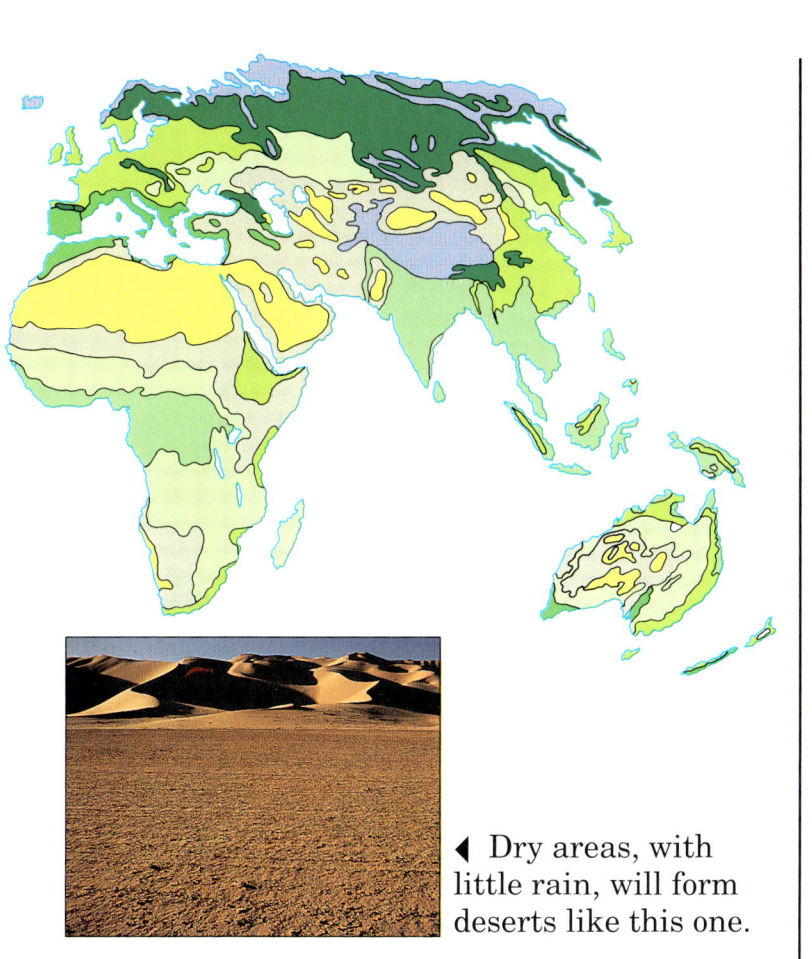

◀ Dry areas, with little rain, will form deserts like this one.

▲ Ice desert in Greenland, where little can grow.

▲ Grassland can thrive where trees do not grow.

▲ Semideserts have hardy plants like cactuses.

▲ Mediterranean scrub has dense, woody shrubs.

hot, wet climate of the tropics, forest trees grow very tall. These rain forests have the greatest number of different kinds of plants in the world. Just as moving toward the poles makes climate cooler, so does rising above sea level. In the high Himalayas, snow covers the mountains all year, even though they lie as close to the equator as Florida. A tall mountain will have a tree line — above this line, trees cannot grow.

39

CLIMATE

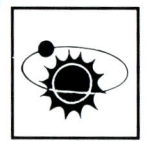

Climate and Animals

This desert rat, or jerboa, from Africa, burrows in the ground to escape the Sun's heat. It hunts for food in the cool nights. Other animals make their homes underground to hide from enemies or to be warm in cold areas.

Just as plants do, animals fit themselves to their climates. In places with cold winters, animals like bears have heavy fur. Some animals, like the Arctic fox, grow white fur in winter to help them hide against the snowy landscape. Many animals go into a deep sleep during winter months. This is called hibernation.

Seasonal Travelers

To avoid winters, some animals move to a warmer climate until spring. For example, many birds fly south for the winter.

◀ These camels are adapted to desert life. The humps on their backs store fat, and they can go for days without food or water.

They come north again to feed in spring. The Arctic tern makes the longest trip of all. This bird spends summer in the Arctic, then flies toward summer in the Antarctic! In desert areas, some animals dig down to cooler sand to escape the heat.

▲ Top: An ermine in its summer coat. Above: In winter, the ermine grows a white coat to help it hide.

This dormouse will hibernate all winter. ▼

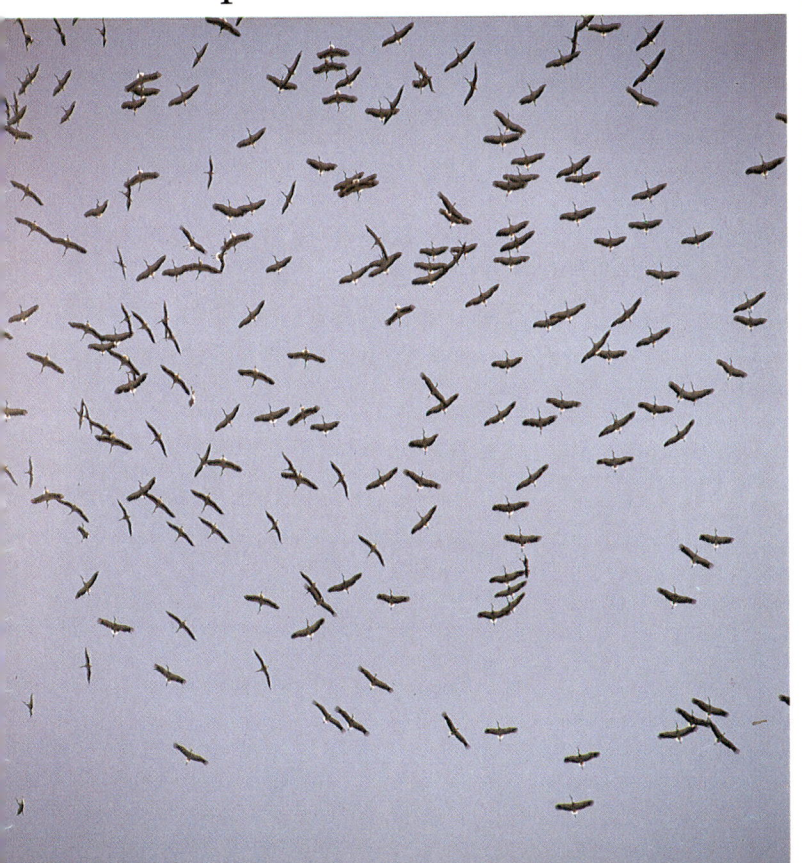

◀ A flock of storks getting ready to fly south for the winter season.

41

5: CHANGES IN CLIMATE

Studying Climate Changes

▲ A nilometer shows the Nile River water level.

Old Instruments

The thermometer was invented in 1592, the barometer in 1643, and rain and wind gauges in the 1600s. Thousands of years ago, the nilometer was invented. This was a simple gauge carved in stone in many places along the Nile River, and it measured how high the river flooded.

We can see climate changes going on in many places right now. For example, monsoon winds bring rain to Asia and Africa. But since the 1960s, winds began changing, bringing much less rain than before. So crops have died in large parts of Africa, and people have starved. In order to better predict such climate changes, we need to know more about how climate has changed in the past.

Changes in the Past

Scientists have kept weather records for about 300 years. To go farther back, we must piece clues together. Old books, letters, and diaries sometimes tell about past weather. Nature also gives us clues. Tree rings show how much rain fell in a year, and lake-bottom mud can show us if the plants that grew there long ago were warm-weather plants or cold-weather plants. To study water temperatures of the distant past, scientists drill core samples from the bottom of the ocean and look at the fossilized shells.

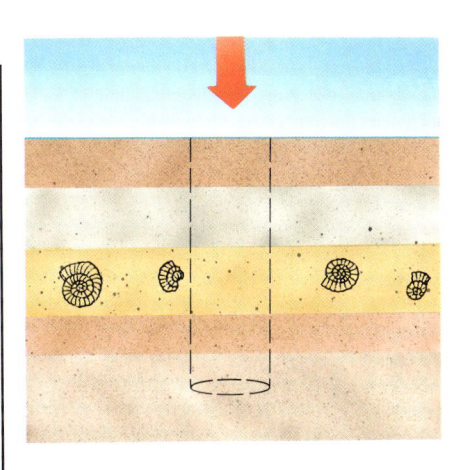

▲ Core samples are drilled from rock layers millions of years old. The fossils in the layers tell about past climates.

This stump has wide and thin rings that show how much the tree grew each year. Wide rings show years of heavy rain, when the tree grew more than in drier years, shown by thin rings. ▼

◀ Four years before this picture was taken, crops grew in this part of India. But the monsoon winds no longer bring rain, and the land is becoming desert.

43

CHANGES IN CLIMATE

Ice Ages

The Evidence

We can find many clues that help us discover when glaciers covered the world. Sedimentary rocks made up of layers of dirt and mud laid down in water over millions of years give us clues. In these layers we can see when plants grew and when they died out. Wide valleys dug by glaciers show that thick ice was once there.

In the past two billion years, for long periods large areas of land were covered with glaciers — thick sheets of ice. These times were ice ages. Today, 10% of Earth's land is covered by ice. In the past, ice covered as much as half of all the world's land.

Glacials

The last Ice Age started two million years ago. Glaciers covered northern Europe, Siberia, and North America. Plants could not grow there. Without plants, animals couldn't live there, either. During glacial periods, the ice kept spreading. During interglacial periods,

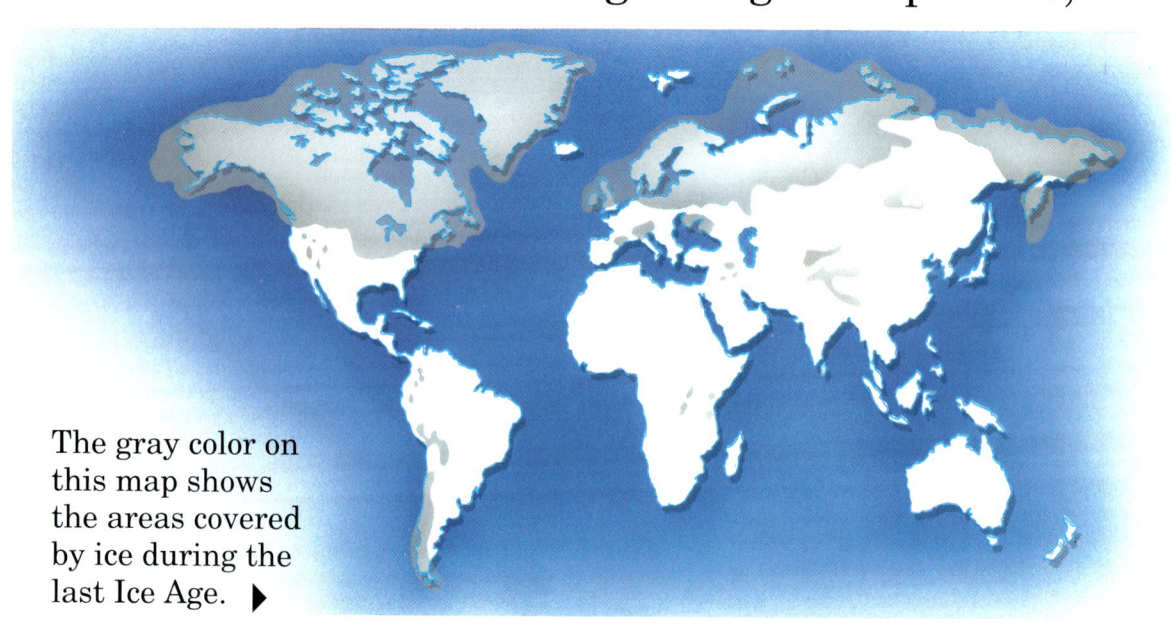

The gray color on this map shows the areas covered by ice during the last Ice Age. ▶

44

◀ This valley in England has a U-shaped floor, showing that a glacier carved it out.

Did You Know?
Earth had six major ice ages before the last one, at about 2.3 billion, 950 million, 750 million, 650 million, 450 million, and 290 million years ago.

the ice melted back. The last interglacial period started 10,000 years ago, and we are still in it. In the coldest periods, so much water froze that the level of the oceans dropped by 460 feet (140 m). Alaska and Siberia were joined by dry land. So were Britain and Europe.

A glacier of today. This slow-moving river of ice is in the Swiss Alps. Studying glaciers helps us learn about ancient climates. ▼

CHANGES IN CLIMATE

Climate in Early Times

Where early peoples went and what they did tells us about the climates they lived in. During the Ice Age, early peoples moved into Australia and North America. Cave paintings made near the end of the Ice Age in France and Spain show that the people hunted rhinoceroses, mammoths, and deer in the warmer weather of that time.

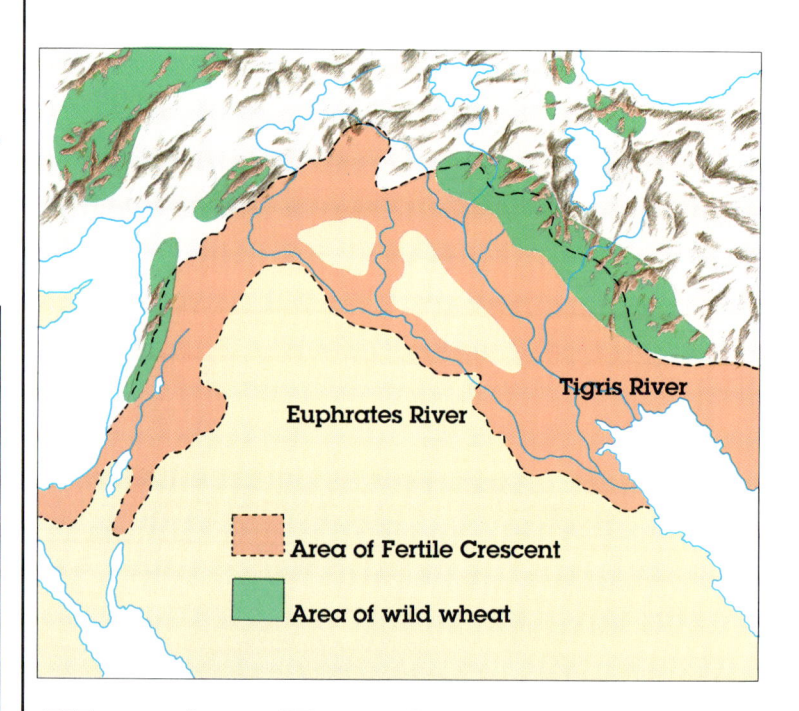

This map shows where wild wheat grew and where people later planted wheat in the Fertile Crescent. Our modern wheat comes from the wild wheat these early farmers raised. ▶

Carbon-14 Dating

Scientists can tell the age of an old object, such as a bone or piece of wood, by finding the amount of radioactive carbon-14 left in it. All living things take in both carbon and carbon-14 atoms. After they die, the carbon-14 decays at a constant rate. Experts measure the amount that is left, and can tell how old animal and plant remains are. The carbon-14 "calendar" can go back more than 50,000 years!

Warming Trends

As the weather got warmer, wild wheat began to grow near the Fertile Crescent in the Middle East. People then began to plant the wheat, and so became farmers. About 5,000 years ago,

46

China had a very warm period when bamboo grew far to the north and many warm-weather animals, such as elephants, lived there. In Pakistan, experts have found city ruins, showing that there was once a great deal of rain in the Indus Valley — enough rain for farms and cities to thrive. Today, this valley gets little rain. People in Europe and North America also enjoyed warm weather and clear skies. This was the warmest the Earth has ever been after the Ice Ages. Since then, it has grown cooler. Around AD 300, a long warm

▲ The Ring of Brodgar, on Orkney Island, was once used to study the night sky. Long ago, skies were clearer than they are now.

▲ These ruins of the great city of Mohenjo-Daro, in the Indus Valley, now face a dry, desertlike climate. But 4,000 years ago, there was plenty of water for crops, animals, and people here.

CHANGES IN CLIMATE

Climate from the Middle Ages

period began in the north. It warmed up to south of the Mediterranean, and south of Virginia. This warmer weather may have helped the Maya Empire grow in North and Central America. In the 900s, the Norse colonized Greenland. But in the Middle East, this warm weather dried up farms.

Frost Fair Facts

During the cold period called the Little Ice Age, England's winters were cold enough to freeze the Thames River. People held Frost Fairs out on the ice, with hundreds of booths. The pillars of Old London Bridge acted like a dam, holding back ice and helping the river freeze, 30 times in all. The river has not frozen since Old London Bridge was torn down in 1831.

The Little Ice Age

From 1400 to 1800, the world had a much cooler period, called the Little Ice Age. Greenland became so cold that Norse settlements came to an end. The wine records kept in Germany and France since the 1300s tell of the cold. In the seventeenth century, farms in Scandinavia were abandoned. The mid-1800s had a short warm period. But in 1879, cold weather brought famine to China and India. Finally, the 1920s saw a return of global warmth. Recent weather changes make some experts say that the climate is getting cooler. But other experts say the Earth is warming up.

The Potato Famine

In 1845, a warm, wet period helped spread a disease that rotted the potato crop in Ireland. Potatoes were the main food for many, and in five years a million people starved to death. By 1861, two million had left for the United States.

◀◀ These incidents show how the world's climate has changed over the last 2,000 years.

1. The Maya culture thrived when the climate was warmer, from 250 AD to 900 AD.
2. Erik the Red brought settlers to Greenland when the warm climate allowed food crops to grow on the island.
3. In the 1300s, severe storms caused flooding in many areas in northern Europe.
4. The Frost Fair of 1683-84 was the largest of the many fairs held when the Thames River froze over during the Little Ice Age.
5. In 1845, warm, wet weather allowed the potato blight to spread, causing starvation.
6. In the late 1800s, the Baltic Sea froze over and people could walk from Sweden to Denmark!

49

CHANGES IN CLIMATE

The Moving Deserts

The yellow areas of this map show where deserts are now. The brown areas show the regions that are in danger of becoming deserts. People speed up this process by clearing away plants and not taking care of the land. ▼

Rock paintings in Africa tell us about the climate before the Sahara Desert formed there. About 5,500 years ago, paintings were made of antelope, deer, crocodiles, elephants, and giraffes. This shows us that there was much more rain there at one time. One picture shows people hunting hippopotamuses from a canoe! Where there is sand now, rivers once flowed. Herds of animals fed on vast grasslands. But when the Ice Age ended, the rains moved farther south. The land dried up and turned into desert. Today, the Sahara is moving into the grasslands south of it. Rainfall

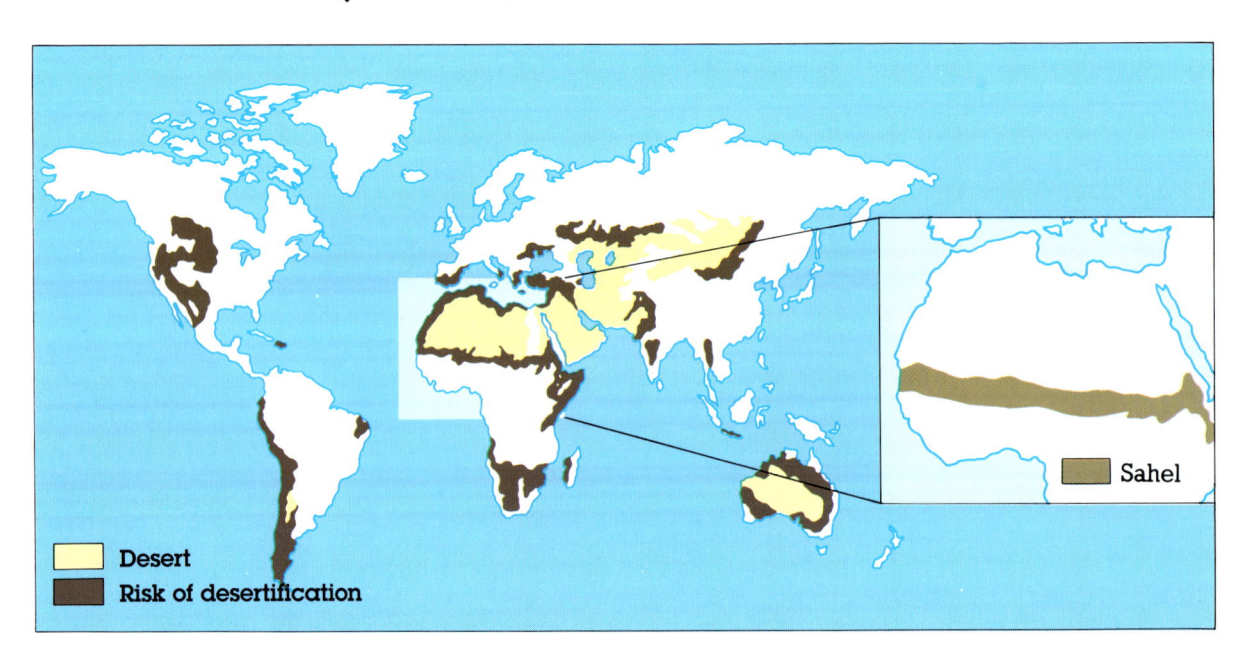

Desert
Risk of desertification

Sahel

▲ A rock painting from a mountain in the Sahara Desert. It shows people tending cattle in what was once grassland.

is unreliable in this region. Terrible famines have struck Ethiopia and Sudan in recent years, causing widespread starvation. The map shows other regions that are in danger of turning into desert from drought and human actions.

Did You Know?

The desert sand of the Sahara sometimes blows as far away as England, leaving a film of fine red dust over everything.

◀ People herding cattle in the Sahel, just south of the Sahara Desert. Rain is becoming scarce there, and the desert is moving in.

51

6: PEOPLE AND CLIMATE

How People Change Climate

Throughout the history of our planet, climate has changed several times from natural causes. But in the last 200 years, people have been able to change the climate. In that time, the number of people in the world has grown from less than one billion humans to around 5.3 billion!

Polluting the Air

Industry has grown hugely in the last two centuries. This results in large amounts of harmful chemicals and other pollutants being pumped into

Acid Rain Facts

Chemical wastes from cars and factories rise into the air, traveling hundreds of miles. They mix with the moisture in the clouds and turn into acids. Then these acids fall to the Earth in the rain, ruining buildings, lakes, plants, and soils. Parts of eastern North America, Europe, and Asia have the worst damage from acid rain.

◀ The Dust Bowl of the 1930s. Huge dust storms buried roads, houses, and livestock.

The Dust Bowl

People can change the climate by changing the plants that grow there. In the Great Plains of the United States, farmers plowed up the native grasses that bound the soil. They planted wheat, which did not bind the soil. During the drought of the 1930s, strong winds blew away the loose soil in huge clouds.

◀◀ Opposite: Trees killed by acid fog in Germany.

Mexico City, one of the world's largest cities, covered with smog. The city lies in a valley that traps air pollution. ▼

the air we breathe. Smoke and fog together make smog — a smelly air condition that can be dangerous to plants, animals, and humans. In large cities like Mexico City, Los Angeles, and Denver, industry and cars have caused severe smog. And our air is getting worse in another way. Like all plants, forest trees breathe in carbon dioxide and give off oxygen, which humans and animals need. By cutting down forests, we are destroying our sources for fresh oxygen. There are half as many forests now as there used to be.

PEOPLE AND CLIMATE

The Greenhouse Effect

Top, right: This iron and steel factory in China pours smoke from fossil fuels into the air. This adds carbon dioxide to the air and helps warm up the Earth.

Coal, oil, and natural gas are called fossil fuels because they are made from decayed plants and animals that died millions of years ago. When we burn these fossil fuels, they give off carbon dioxide gas. We have put a great deal of this gas into our atmosphere since the Industrial Revolution in the 1700s. Carbon dioxide lets the Sun's warm rays reach the Earth. But it traps most of the heat here, the way a greenhouse traps heat for the plants growing inside it. This is called the greenhouse effect, and it is making our planet grow warmer. Other gases that act the same way are CFCs — chlorofluorocarbons — that are used in refrigerators and have been used in spray cans.

What Are CFCs?

CFCs are chemicals, chlorofluorocarbons, that contain chlorine, fluorine, and carbon. They have no odor or color and they do not burn. They have trade names like Freon, Arcton, and Geon. They are used in air conditioners, in refrigerators, and in some spray cans. They are also used in foam packages and insulation.

In Europe, some glaciers are shrinking, and the Southern Hemisphere is also warming up. The Earth may be having one of its natural warm periods. But many scientists think human activities are increasing the greenhouse effect. If we do not change our actions, the results could be disastrous.

Warm Results

If the greenhouse effect is not stopped, the ice caps will melt and the seas will rise to flood coastal areas. Cities like Los Angeles, London, Tokyo, and Montreal would drown. Rainfall patterns may shift. Some areas now green may become deserts; some deserts may be flooded. Frozen areas of Canada and Siberia may turn milder.

Sun's rays

Atmosphere

Earth

The greenhouse effect. The Sun's rays warm the Earth's atmosphere. Carbon dioxide and other gases, shown as a blue band, may keep most of this warmth from leaving our atmosphere. The Sun keeps sending more heat, so the Earth gets warmer and warmer. ▶

PEOPLE AND CLIMATE

The Ozone Layer

A Protective Shield

The Earth's atmosphere forms a shield that protects us from the harmful rays of the Sun. The ozone layer makes up part of this shield. Ozone is a blue gas made up of three oxygen atoms. Near the ground, ozone can help form smog and is harmful. But high in the atmosphere, ozone

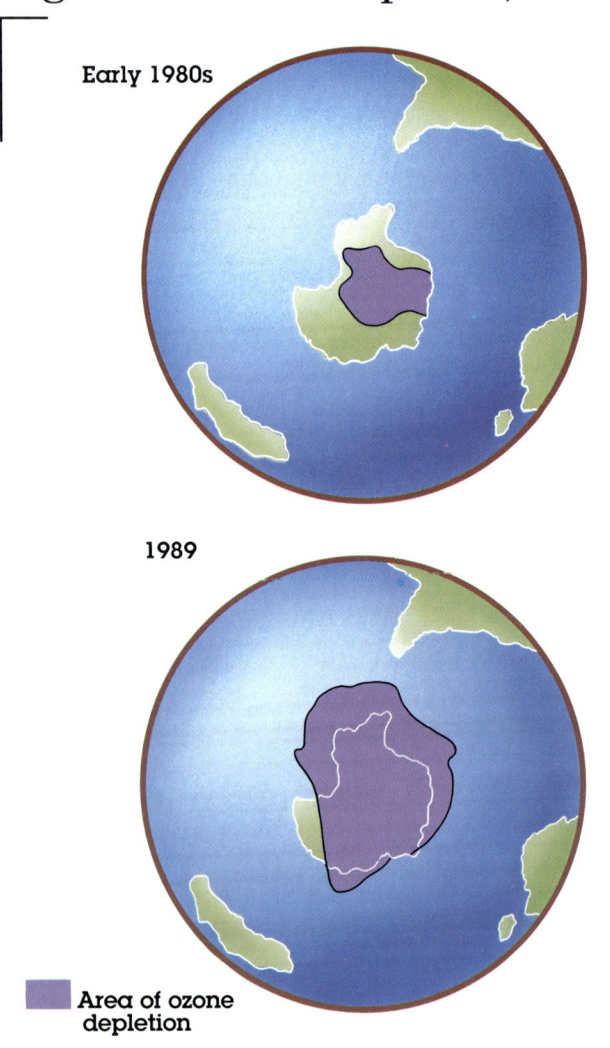

The top picture shows the Antarctic ozone hole in 1980. The bottom picture shows how the hole had spread over the continent of Antarctica by 1989. ▶

Early 1980s

1989

Area of ozone depletion

The Dangers

So far, the ozone holes are over regions where very few humans live. But if holes develop over populated areas, there will be more skin cancer, cataracts, and blindness. Some other diseases will also spread more easily. Acid smog might form. Food plants, such as rice, would not grow as well, leading to short supplies.

protects us from ultraviolet rays that can cause cancer.

The Ozone Hole

In the 1980s, scientists working in Antarctica discovered that a hole was forming in the ozone layer above Antarctica. Each year, the hole is growing larger. Now, another hole has opened up over the Arctic. What caused these holes? Scientists suspect that CFCs caused them. These are the same chemicals that help cause the greenhouse effect. In 1990, 50 countries signed a treaty, agreeing to stop making CFCs. But CFCs last up to 140 years. So the ozone holes will be with us for a long time.

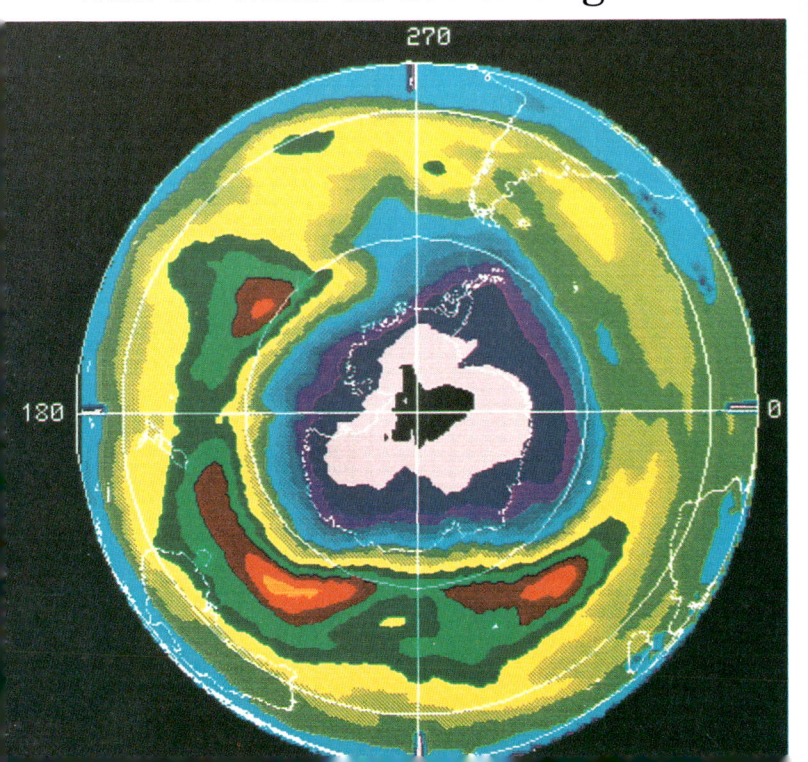

Friendly to Ozone?

The United States no longer uses CFCs in spray cans. Now most other nations will also stop. But there still may be many CFC spray cans in the warehouses and stores in some countries. To be sure of using an ozone-safe can, read the label first. Better yet, use pump sprays.

▲ Scientists working at the British Antarctic Survey Station first detected the ozone hole.

◀ A picture taken by the US *Nimbus-7* satellite of the spreading ozone hole that now covers all of the Antarctic. The center of the hole is black. Pink and purple show areas that have some ozone.

57

PEOPLE AND CLIMATE

Climate in the Future

These fishing boats on ▶ the shore of the Aral Sea have been left to rust and rot. The water now lies several miles away and the fish have died out.

Global Warming

If global warming keeps up, we might face many changes in the way we live. Summers would be hotter, so more people may use air conditioners, which would make the ozone problem worse. Water would be rationed. Food would cost much more because crops need water to grow. More forests would turn dry and burn, and floods would follow.

The world's climate is changing. But it is hard to tell if it is cooling down or warming up. Africa's droughts and starvation may be part of the change.

The Action Needed

We must watch climate changes to see how they will affect our food supplies. Studying past climates will help us decide what may happen in the future. We must take steps to be sure of getting food in unfavorable weather. At the same time, we must not upset the climate in any other way. For example, the

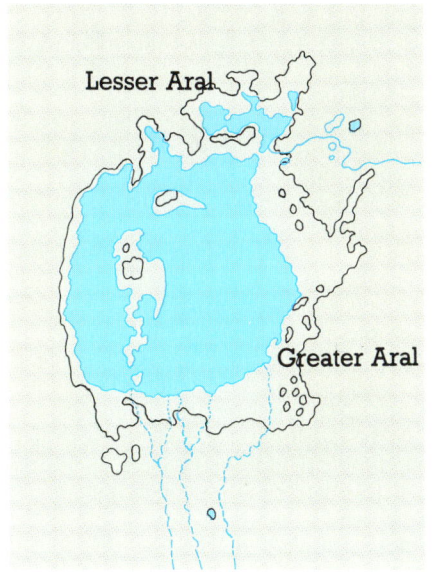

▲ The Aral Sea today, after splitting into two parts. The 1961 shoreline is outlined in black.

Soviets have been taking water from the rivers that flow into the Aral Sea and using it to irrigate farmland. When the Aral Sea began to shrink, the water got saltier and killed the fish that were a source of food. Now the Soviets want to take water from rivers flowing into the Arctic Ocean. But without the fresh river water, the ocean might not form ice. This would warm the climate and bring drought to Europe and central Asia. Since climate affects everyone, we need to see all the steps ahead before making changes.

▲ These starving people of Mali are being fed in a relief camp. Crops die in droughts that strike large sections of Africa.

Glossary

Air masses: Bodies of air that move constantly all over the world.

Anemometer: An instrument that measures how fast the wind is blowing. A simple anemometer has several metal cups on spokes that are attached to a shaft. The shaft is linked to dials. When the wind spins the cups, its speed can be read from the dials.

Aneroid: Not using liquid. An aneroid barometer has a needle connected to the top of a small box that has had some of its air taken out. A change in air pressure moves the box lid up and down, and this moves the needle. The air pressure can be read from the needle's position on a scale.

Anticyclone: An area of high pressure. The winds of an anticyclone blow in a spiral outward from the center.

Asteroids: Cold, rocky bodies smaller than planets that orbit the Sun between Mars and Jupiter.

Atmosphere: The layer of gases, or air, that surrounds the Earth. The atmosphere is made up mostly of the gases nitrogen and oxygen.

Atom: The smallest amount of an element. Each element is made up of one kind of atom, which is different from the atoms of all other elements.

Axis: A line around which something turns or rotates. The Earth rotates around an axis that runs through it from the North Pole to the South Pole.

Barometer: An instrument for measuring air pressure. A mercury barometer uses a long glass tube filled with mercury. When the air pressure changes, the mercury goes up or down inside the tube. An aneroid barometer uses a small metal box that moves a needle on a scale to show air pressure.

Carbon dioxide: A colorless, odorless gas given out by animals when they breathe. This gas is taken in by plants, which give out oxygen.

Carbon-14 dating: A method of finding out how old an object is by measuring the amount of carbon-14 left in it. This dating method can be used only for samples that were once part of a living plant or animal. Examples include charcoal, bones, shells, and similar materials.

Chlorofluorocarbons (CFCs): Chemicals made up from the elements chlorine, fluorine, and carbon. CFCs can damage the ozone layer.

Condense: To change from a gas, or vapor, to a liquid. An example is when steam condenses into water.

Core: A long, thin sample of rock or soil that was taken by a hollow drill.

Crater: A hollow left after a meteorite strikes the ground, or a hollow left in a volcano after it has erupted.

Crystal: A solid that has a regular shape. Some examples are sugar, salt, and snowflakes.

Cyclone: An area of low pressure, where the winds blow in a spiral inward toward the center.

Dense: Thick; having parts that are crowded or packed together; difficult to get through, like shrubbery growing very close together.

Depression: Another name for a cyclone.

Evaporation: The change from a liquid or a solid to a vapor, or gas.

Fossil fuels: Fuels made from the remains of plants and animals over millions of years. Coal, oil, and natural gas are fossil fuels.

Fossilized: A word describing ancient plant or animal remains changed into a stony form that has been preserved in rocks.

Front: The boundary between two air masses that have different temperatures.

Helium: A very light, colorless gas that does not burn. It is often used to make balloons float.

Hemisphere: Half a globe. The equator divides the Earth into the Northern and Southern hemispheres.

High: A short name for an area of high pressure. It is also called an anticyclone.

Himalayas: A very long mountain range north of India. This range contains the highest mountains in the world.

Humidity: The amount of water vapor in the air.

Hurricane: A violent storm that is made by a tropical cyclone.

Hydrogen: A gas that is the lightest chemical element. It can float balloons, but it burns very easily.

Ice Age: A time in the Earth's past when large areas of the world's land were covered by thick ice. There were several ice ages, but only the last one is known as the Ice Age. This Ice Age took place during the Pleistocene epoch, from 2.5 million years to about 10,000 years ago.

Ice caps: Thick sheets of ice covering large areas of land, especially in Antarctica and Greenland. Sheets like these covered much larger areas during ice ages.

Industrial Revolution: The rapid development of machines and factories that replaced hand-crafted goods in Great Britain, Europe, and the United States during the eighteenth and nineteenth centuries.

Isobars: Lines connecting points of equal pressure on a weather map.

Latitudes: Regions of the Earth that lie north or south of the equator, marked on maps by imaginary lines. The higher the latitude, the farther north or south it is from the equator.

Low: A short name for an area of low pressure, or a cyclone.

Magnetic field: The area of force that surrounds a magnet. A magnetic field surrounds Earth, but it is weakest at the poles.

Mercury: A silver-colored metal that is a liquid at normal temperatures. It is often used in thermometers and barometers.

Meteorite: A lump of metallic or rocky material from outer space that lands on the Earth.

Middle Ages: The period of European history between ancient and modern times, from about AD 500 to 1500.

Monsoon: A wind that changes direction according to the season. Also, the rains that it brings to certain parts of the world in summer.

Norse: Concerning ancient Scandinavia or the culture of the Norsemen who lived there.

Nuclear: A word referring to the nucleus, or core, of an atom. This nucleus contains enormous energy.

Observatory: A place or building where people study the stars and planets. Observatories of today use cameras linked with high-powered tracking telescopes.

Ozone: A kind of oxygen whose molecules have three oxygen atoms instead of the usual two. In our atmosphere, ozone shields Earth from the Sun's dangerous rays. On Earth's surface, ozone is harmful to all life.

Pleistocene epoch: A period of Earth's history that began 2.5 million years ago and ended about 10,000 years ago. The Ice Age took place during this time.

Precipitation: A word that describes rain, hail, sleet, and snow.

Radar: A device that bounces radio waves off an object in order to measure the distance to it and to keep track of its movements.

Radiation: The flow of particles and rays, such as light and radio waves. It also means the energy released from an atom.

Radioactive: Giving out atomic energy. Radioactivity can be harmful or harmless, short-lived or long-lived. These things depend on which elements are radioactive.

Rain forests: Forests growing in tropical areas that have heavy rainfall.

Sedimentary rock: Rock that was formed from layers of tiny particles of other rock.

Sonde: An instrument for measuring and sending back information on weather or other conditions high above the Earth's surface. Sondes are sent aloft on weather balloons.

Static electricity: Electricity that does not flow. Instead, it builds up until it discharges in a spark. Current electricity is the type that flows, the kind used to light buildings.

Temperate: A climate between polar cold and tropical heat. Earth has two temperate zones. On a map, the temperate zones lie between 23.5° and 66.5° north and south of the equator.

Tides: The regular rise and fall of the ocean levels, caused by the Moon's pull on the water.

Tropics: The zones around the Earth on both sides of the equator. The climate in these areas is very warm or hot all year round. Tropics often have heavy rainfall.

Vapor: Particles of moisture or solids that form clouds or smoke. Air can hold moisture that you cannot see.

Index

A **boldface** number shows that the entry is illustrated on that page. The same page often has text about the entry, too.

acid rain and fog **52**, 53
acid smog 56
agriculture, start of **46**
air masses 27 (*see also* fronts)
air pressure 6, 7, 12, 13, 17, **20**
alpine climates **38-39**
altocumulus clouds **9**
anemometers (wind-speed indicators) **28**, 29
animals and climate 24, 36, **40-41**
Antarctic Circle 4
Antarctica 38, **57**
anticyclones (high-pressure areas) **12**, **22**, **23**
aphelion 34
Aral Sea **58-59**
Arctic Circle 4
Arctic fox 40
Arctic tern 41
asteroids, near misses of 36
astronomical observatories, early 47
atmosphere, dust in **36-37**
auroras (flickering lights) **35**
autumn (*see* seasons)

backing winds 13
balloons, weather 17, 18, **19**
Baltic Sea, freezing of **49**
Bangladesh 14
barometers **7**, 42
Barringer Meteor Crater 36
beaches
    near the Arctic Circle **4-5**
    in the tropics **5**
Beaufort wind scale 29
breezes, coastal **13**
broad-leaved forests **38-39**

camels **41**
camouflage, animal 40, **41**
carbon dioxide 53, 54, 55
carbon-14 dating 46
cave paintings 46
CFCs (chlorofluorocarbons) 54, 56, 57
changes, climatic 5
    in early times 46-47
    and Earth-Sun position 34
    in the future 54-55, 58-59
    of the Ice Age **44-45**
    of the Little Ice Age **48**, 49

from the Middle Ages **48-49**
and moving deserts **50**-51
studying 42-43
(*see also* pollution)
charts, weather 20, **21**, **22-23**
cirrus clouds **8-9**
climate 4-5, 24-41
    animals and 24, 36, **40-41**
    changes in 5, 34, **42-51**, 55, **58-59**
    factors making up **32-33**
    main types of **24-25**
    people and **52-59**
    plants and 24, 33, **38-39**, 43
    sea and land and **6-7**, **26-**27, 33, **58-59**
    and the seasons **30-31**, 32
    and the Sun 11, 32, **33-**35
    and volcanoes and meteorites **36-37**
    and winds **28-29**
    worldwide **24-25**
clouds 7, **8-9**, 17, 33
    and jet streams 29
CN Tower 15
coastal regions (*see* breezes, coastal *and* land and sea)
cold fronts (*see* fronts)
cold sea currents 26
communications in weather forecasting 18-19, **20-21**
    (*see also* satellites, weather)
computers in weather forecasting 18-19, 20, **21**
condensation **6**, **7**, **8**, 11
coniferous forests **38-39**
continental moist climate **24-25**
cores, ocean-bed **43**
Cosigüina 36, 37
country lore 16
cumulonimbus clouds **9**, 15
cumulus clouds 8, **9**
currents, ocean and sea **26**-27, 33
    direction of 27
cyclones (low-pressure areas) **12**, **22**, **23** (*see also* tornadoes *and* tropical storms)

depressions (*see* low-pressure areas)
desert climates **24-25**, **38-39**, **40**, **41**
desert rat (*see* jerboa)
desertification **50-51**
dew 11
dinosaurs, extinction of 36
direction
    of ocean currents 27
    of winds 29
doldrums **28**

dormouse **41**
drizzle 10, **22**
droughts 42, 43, 48, 50-51, 58, **59**
dust (*see* pollution *and* volcanoes)
Dust Bowl **52-53**

Eiffel Tower **9**
El Niño (sea current) 27
equator 4, 6, **7**, 25, 26, 32
equatorial rain forest **38-39**
Erik the Red 49
Eriksson, Leif 48, 49
ermine **41**
evaporation **6**, 7, 8

fall (*see* seasons)
famines 42, 49, 51, 58, **59**
Fertile Crescent 46
fog 8, 22 (*see also* smog)
forecasts, weather **16-23**
    obtaining data for 16-17, **18-21**
    putting together **20-21**
    radar, balloons, and satellites and **12**, **18-19**, **21**, **57**
    reading maps for **22-23**
    special 22
forests **38-39**, 53
fossil fuels 5, 54 (*see also* pollution)
fossils 43
fronts 7, **22**, **23**, 27, 29
frost 11, 22
Frost Fairs **48**, 49

glacial periods (*see* ice ages)
global warming 54, **55-57**, 58
grasslands **38-39**
greenhouse effect **54-55**
Greenland 39, **48**, 49
groundhog 16
Gulf Stream **26**-27

hail 7, 10, 11
haze
    industrial 33
    volcanic **36-37**
    (*see also* mist *and* smog)
heat gains and losses 32-**33**
    (*see also* global warming)
Hermes (asteroid) 36
hibernation 40, **41**
highland climate **24-25**
high-pressure areas **12**, **22**, **23**
highs (*see* high-pressure areas)
horse latitudes **28**
humidity 17
hurricanes (*see* tropical storms)

62

ice ages
  Ice Age (Pleistocene epoch) 5, **44-45**
  Little Ice Age **48**, 49
ice caps **24-25**, **33**, **44**, 55
ice deserts **38-39**
Indus Valley **47**
Industrial Revolution 54
instruments, weather **17**, 18-**19**, **42** (*see also names of specific instruments*)
interglacials (*see* ice ages)
isobars **20**, **22**, **23**

jerboa (desert rat) **40**
jet streams **29**

Kenya, Mount **25**

land and sea **6**, 7, **26**-27
  (*see also* breezes, coastal)
lightning **15**
Little Ice Age **48**, 49
London Bridge, Old 48
low-pressure areas **12**, 14, **22**, **23**
lows (*see* low-pressure areas)

maps
  of climatic regions **24-25**, **38-39**
  TV weather **22**, **23**
  (*see also* weather: maps)
Maya civilization **48**, 49
Mediterranean scrub **38-39**
meteorites 36
Mexico City **53**
migration **40-41**
mist **8**, **22**
Mohenjo-Daro **47**
monsoon winds, failure of **42-43**

nilometers **42**
nimbus clouds **9**
Nimbus 7 (satellite) 57
NOAA-9 (satellite) 12
Norse settlements **48**-49

observatories, early (*see* astronomical observatories, early)
occluded fronts **22**, **27**
ocean currents **26-27**, 33
oceanic moist climate **24-25**
orbit, Earth's
  and distance from Sun **34**
  and seasons 30, **31**
ozone layer **56-57**

people and climate 5, 51, **52-59**
  and the future 58-59
  and the greenhouse effect **54-55**

and the ozone layer **56-57**
perihelion **34**
plants, climate and 24, 33, **38-39**, 43
polar circles **4**
polar climate **24-25**
pollution 5, 33, 36, **52-53**
  and the greenhouse effect **54-55**
  and the ozone layer **56-57**
population, world 52
Potato Famine, Irish **49**
prairies (*see* grasslands)
precipitation (*see* hail, rain, *and* snow)
pressure (*see* air pressure)
prevailing winds **28-29**
protective skin coloring 25 (*see also* camouflage, animal)

radar 18, **19**
radiation balance 32-33, 54, **55**
radio telescope **28**
radiosondes 18, **19**
rain **6**, 10-**11**, **22**, **23**, 35, 47
  monsoon **42-43**
  (*see also* droughts)
rain forests **38-39**, 53
rain shadow **11**
rainbows **10**
red dust 51
reflected heat 32-**33**, **55**
reflected sunlight 33
reporting, weather **16-21**
Ring of Brodgar **47**
rock paintings 50, **51**

Sahara Desert **39**, **50**, 51
Sahel **50**, **51**
St. Helens, Mount 36
satellites, weather 12, **18-19**, **21**, 57
sea and land **6**, 7, **26-27**, **33**, **58-59**
seasons 5, **30-31**, **32**
  animals' adaptations to 40-**41**
sedimentary rocks **44**
semideserts **38-39** (*see also* Sahel)
shadow, rain **11**
ships, weather **17**
showers **22**, **23** (*see also* rain)
skin coloring, protective 25 (*see also* camouflage, animal)
Skylab 34
slopes, north- and south-facing **32**, 33
smog 8, **52**, **53**, 56
snow 7, 10, 11, **23**, **32**, **33**, 39
snowflakes **11**
solar flares (*see* solar prominences)

solar power stations **33**
solar prominences **34**
solar wind 34
sondes (*see* radiosondes)
soot 36
space watch **18-19**, **29**, **34** (*see also* satellites, weather)
spray cans 54, 56, 57
spring (*see* seasons)
static electricity **15**
steppe climate **24-25**
storks, white **41**
storms **14-15**
  thunderstorms 10, 15
stratus clouds 8, **9**
subarctic climate **24-25**
subtropical climates **24-25**
summer (*see* seasons)
Sun 6, 7, 11, **34-35**
  and aurora borealis **35**
  and radiation balance 32, **33**
  and seasons 30, **31**
  and sunspots **34-35**
  and "Turner sunsets" **37**
symbols on weather maps **22-23**, 27

temperate lands and climates **38-39**
temperature 7, 8, 43
  measuring **17**, 42
  (*see also* climate, global warming, ice ages, *and* weather)
thermometers **17**, 42
thunderclouds **9**
thunderstorms 10, 15
tides 26
tornadoes **14-15**
trade winds **28**
trees
  in fall 30-**31**
  ring patterns of **43**
  in summer **30**
  and tree lines 39
Tri-State Tornado 14
Tropic of Cancer **4**
Tropic of Capricorn **4**
tropical climates **24-25**, **38-39**
tropical rain forests **38-39**, 53
tropical storms **14-15**
tropics 4, 5
tundra **38-39**
Turner, Joseph 37
typhoons (*see* tropical storms)

ultraviolet rays 57

valleys, U-shaped **45**
veering winds 13

63

vegetation, types of **38-39**
volcanoes **36-37**

warm fronts (*see* fronts)
warm sea currents **26**
    El Niño 27
water cycle **6**, 7, 8
weather
    balloons 17, 18, **19**
    and climate 4-5
    factors behind **6-15**
    forecasting the **16-23**
    maps **20**, **22-23**
    networks for forecasting **18-19**
    ships **17**
    (*see also names of specific
        kinds of weather*)
wheat, origin of 46
white storks **41**
willy-willies (*see* tropical storms)
wind(s) **11** , 17, **22**, **28-29**, 33
    direction of 29
    and highs and lows **12**-13
    monsoon **42-43**
    prevailing **28-29**
    solar 34
    and storms **14-15**
winter (*see* seasons)